## What Every Teacher Should Know About

# Instructional Planning

W0008379

# What Every Teacher Should Know About ...

DONNA WALKER TILESTON

# What Every Teacher Should Know About

# INSTRUCTIONAL PLANNING

**CORWIN PRESS**
A Sage Publications Company
Thousand Oaks, California

*For information:*

Corwin Press
A Sage Publications Company
2455 Teller Road
Thousand Oaks, California 91320
www.corwinpress.com

Sage Publications Ltd.
6 Bonhill Street
London EC2A 4PU
United Kingdom

Sage Publications India Pvt. Ltd.
B-42, Panchsheel Enclave
Post Box 4209
New Delhi 110 017  India

Printed in the United States of America

**Library of Congress Cataloging-in-Publication Data**

Tileston, Donna Walker.
What every teacher should know about instructional
planning / Donna Walker Tileston.
    p. cm. — (What every teacher should know about—; 4)
Includes bibliographical references and index.
ISBN 0-7619-3120-1 (pbk.)
    1. Lesson planning. I. Title. II. Series.
LB1027.4.T55 2004
371.3′028—c21                                    2003010807

This book is printed on acid-free paper.

03   04   05   06   10   9   8   7   6   5   4   3

| | |
|---|---|
| *Acquisitions Editor:* | Faye Zucker |
| *Editorial Assistant:* | Stacy Wagner |
| *Production Editor:* | Diane S. Foster |
| *Copy Editor:* | Stacey Shimizu |
| *Typesetter:* | C&M Digitals (P) Ltd. |
| *Proofreader:* | Mary Meagher |
| *Indexer:* | Molly Hall |
| *Cover Designer:* | Tracy E. Miller |
| *Production Artist:* | Lisa Miller |

# Contents

# About the Author

**Donna Walker Tileston,** Ed.D., is a veteran teacher of 27 years and the president of Strategic Teaching and Learning, a consulting firm that provides services to schools throughout the United States and Canada. Also an author, Donna's publications include *Strategies for Teaching Differently: On the Block or Not* (Corwin Press, 1998), *Innovative Strategies of the Block Schedule* (Bureau of Education and Research [BER], 1999), and *Ten Best Teaching Practices: How Brain Research, Learning Styles, and Standards Define Teaching Competencies* (Corwin Press, 2000), which has been on Corwin's best-seller list since its first year in print.

Donna received her B.A. from the University of North Texas, her M.A. from East Texas State University, and her Ed.D. from Texas A & M University-Commerce. She may be reached at www.strategicteachinglearning.com or by e-mail at dwtileston@yahoo.com.

# Acknowledgments

M y sincere thanks go to my Acquisitions Editor, Faye Zucker, for her faith in education and what this information can do to help all children be successful. Without Faye, these books would not have been possible.

I had the best team of editors around: Diane Foster, Stacy Wagner, and Stacey Shimizu. You took my words and you gave them power. Thank you.

Thanks to my wonderful Board Chairman at Strategic Teaching and Learning, Dulany Howland: Thank you for sticking with me in the good times and the tough spots. Your expertise and friendship have been invaluable.

*To my brother, Tim Walker, whose kindness and generosity have been an anchor throughout this project.*

# Introduction

John Steinbeck once wrote of a teacher who had made a difference in his life. He said that her students could not wait for school to begin each day and that they left with a hunger for more. We all aspire to be the kind of teacher that John Steinbeck had, a teacher who inspires beyond the hours of the classroom and who creates a hunger for learning in students. Such a teacher does not come to the classroom ill prepared nor does such a teacher base student success on hope. A teacher of this caliber knows that learning takes a tremendous amount of planning and preplanning—and also knows that there is a pattern to planning that helps assure that the hopes and goals are a reality.

In the 1960s, there was a pervasive belief that schools had little to do with the success of students. Rather, the belief was that the environment from which students came and the resources of that environment had the greatest impact on how well they would do in school. Thanks to the work of such pioneers as Ron Edmonds of the Effective Schools Movement and to the work of brain researchers, we now know that schools, in fact, have a tremendous influence on student success. By understanding and planning for learning differences and by teaching to all of the systems of the brain (i.e., the self-, metacognitive, and cognitive systems), teachers today have a great influence over what students become.

This book will examine ways in which the teacher can be an effective planner who helps students tap into the brain's natural motivation to learn and who provides meaningful learning experiences to the classroom. How to write and implement both declarative and procedural objectives will be explored, as will effective strategies for monitoring student success. Based on a model that requires that the curriculum, the assessment program, and the instructional program to be in perfect alignment, this book will provide a step-by-step guide for implementation.

We know that an understanding of vocabulary is vital to educational achievement. With that in mind, I have provided a list of vocabulary words that will be a part of this book. Form 0.1 provides the vocabulary that will be examined throughout this volume: Look at the words to see which ones are familiar and which are not. Write your own definitions in the middle column, and then review your answers as you read.

In addition, I am providing a vocabulary pre-test for you. After you have read the book, you will be given a post-test and the solutions to the tests. The Vocabulary Summary offers additional information about these words and other terms associated with motivation.

**Form 0.1**    Vocabulary List for Instructional Planning

| Vocabulary Word | Your Definition | Your Revised Definition |
|---|---|---|
| Accountability | | |
| Achievement gap | | |
| Alignment | | |
| Assessment | | |
| Benchmark | | |
| Cognitive development | | |
| Contextualizing | | |
| Cooperative learning | | |
| Curriculum | | |
| Data-based decision making | | |
| Declarative information related to storage | | |
| Declarative objectives | | |
| Enrichment | | |
| Essential questions | | |
| Explicit instruction | | |

(Continued)

**Form 0.1** Continued

| | | |
|---|---|---|
| *Indirect experience* | | |
| *Interdisciplinary curriculum* | | |
| *Mixed-ability grouping* | | |
| *Multi-age grouping* | | |
| *Performance tasks* | | |
| *Pluralizing* | | |
| *Procedural objectives* | | |
| *Reflection activities* | | |
| *Scaffolding* | | |
| *Shaping* | | |
| *Spiral curriculum* | | |
| *Standards* | | |
| *Teaching for understanding* | | |
| *Teaching to the test* | | |

# Vocabulary Pre-Test

**Instructions:** For each question, choose the one best answer.

1. Teaching the 20 words that will be on the spelling test to the exclusion of other spelling words is called . . .
   A. Teaching to the test
   B. Teaching for understanding
   C. Shaping
   D. Explicit teaching

2. A lesson is aligned when . . .
   A. We teach for understanding
   B. We teach to the objectives
   C. We teach and assess to the written curriculum or standards
   D. We use state and local standards as a base for learning

3. What is the term for teaching the same concepts over time with each introduction adding depth to the learning?
   A. Scaffolding
   B. Spiral curriculum
   C. Performance tasks
   D. Teaching for understanding

4. When we look at data to determine if all groups of students are making gains in learning, we have . . .
   A. Differentiated the data
   B. Benchmarked the data
   C. Disaggregated the data
   D. Manipulated the data

5. Essential questions relate to . . .
   A. Dividing units into lessons
   B. Good questioning techniques
   C. Declarative objectives
   D. Procedural objectives

6. Providing opportunities for bright students to work on more complex tasks is called what?
   A. Scaffolding
   B. Performance tasks
   C. Enrichment
   D. Pluralizing

7. Choose the answer that is *not* an example of a phase of procedural knowledge.
   A. Constructing models
   B. Meaning making
   C. Shaping
   D. Internalizing

8. What is the most overlooked phase of procedural knowledge?
   A. Constructing models
   B. Meaning making
   C. Shaping
   D. Internalizing

9. What is the key to internalizing?
   A. Practice
   B. Modeling
   C. Extending
   D. Questioning

10. When we point out to students possible problems they may encounter in the learning, we are using . . .
    A. Extending
    B. Modeling
    C. Shaping
    D. Organizing

11. Nonlinguistic or graphic models are an example of what?
    A. Shaping
    B. Organizing
    C. Extending
    D. Internalizing

12. Giving students many examples and ideas and then gradually giving less directions as students have more opportunities to use the information is an example of . . .
    A. Organizing
    B. Internalizing
    C. Shaping
    D. Scaffolding

13. *Resources, group goals, environment,* and *tasks* are terms used in . . .
    A. Enrichment
    B. Cooperative learning
    C. Differentiated instruction
    D. Interdisciplinary curriculum

14. Which of the pathways is most often used in providing context to the learning?
    A. Procedural
    B. Semantic
    C. Episodic
    D. Automatic

15. Teaching by using a story format is an example of what?
    A. Pluralizing
    B. Contextualizing

    C. Scaffolding

    D. Enrichment

16. When we add movement to learning math facts, we are adding which of the pathways to the learning?
    A. Semantic
    B. Episodic
    C. Enriching
    D. Procedural

17. An example of a procedural objective is . . .
    A. "Students will know the meaning of the vocabulary."
    B. "Students will develop a plan for problem solving."
    C. "Students will know the names of the main characters in the story."
    D. "Students will know the parts to a story."

18. An example of a declarative objective is . . .
    A. "Students will know the parts to a story."
    B. "Students will answer the questions asked by their peers."
    C. "Students will develop a mind map on the parts of a bicycle."
    D. "Students will demonstrate variations and errors."

19. Teachers who provide more than one context when teaching are . . .
    A. Scaffolding
    B. Pluralizing
    C. Using spiral curriculum
    D. Using direct experience

20. Which of the following is *not* true of performance tasks?
    A. They are written for a given audience.
    B. They are real world.
    C. They are procedural.
    D. They are usually teacher driven.

# 1

# The Principles of Planning

As teachers, we devote a great deal of time and thought to the *what* and the *how* of teaching. What will we teach? How should the information be presented? How will we know that students know and can use the information?

Good teaching doesn't just happen; it is well planned and is aligned in several ways. First, the written curriculum, the teaching strategies, and the methods of evaluation are all aligned to each other; that is, we align what we say we are going to teach (i.e., state standards, local standards, curriculum, and classroom objectives) with what we actually teach our students and what we assess them on. This alignment can be shown visually as an equilateral triangle, with all sides being equal in importance and with the student in the middle (see Figure 1.1).

Within each of these factors (curriculum, teaching, and assessment) are microalignments that help assure that all students will know and understand the information. Throughout this book, we will examine this microprocess and the components that help to make it successful.

**Figure 1.1**    The Aligned Curriculum

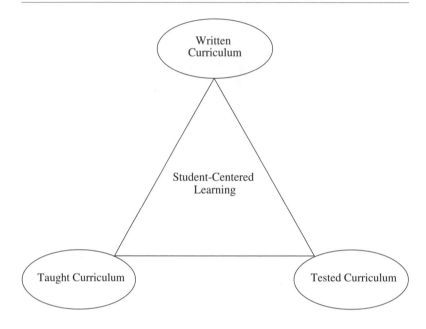

## WHY GOOD PLANNING MAKES FOR
## GOOD LEARNING EXPERIENCES

One of my favorite stories is *Alice in Wonderland*. A much-quoted passage from Alice's adventures is the exchange between Alice and the all-knowing Cheshire cat. Alice is lost and asks the cat for directions. The Cheshire cat asks her which way she is going. Turning, she replies that she is not sure. The cat says that if she does not know where she is going, it does not matter which way she goes. That dialogue provides a perfect model for why good planning makes for good learning experiences. Without planning, it will be difficult to identify where we are going, much less the expected results. For our students' sake, we need to know specifically where we are going with the learning, how we will get there, and what the expected results will be. Through brain research and meta-analysis research on teaching strategies, we can provide a complete map for our students for the first time in history.

Wiggins and McTighe (1998) identify a three-step process in planning for instruction. First, we need to ask what it is that we want students to know and be able to do as a result of the learning. Second, we must examine how we will know that our students are learning and that they can perform tasks as a result of the learning. Third, we must identify which instructional practices will assure us that students learn and that they can use the information provided. Certainly, this complex process shows that teaching should not be left to a hit-or-miss approach.

When we teach using this three-step process, there are no surprises, no "gotchas," in which students are assessed on something for which they have not been taught. Furthermore, by stating objectives up front, telling students and parents how students will be assessed on those objectives, and then teaching those objectives, we become more accountable for student learning. Our objectives, assessment instruments, and teaching strategies become a system leading to quality learning. Should something go wrong with that system, we are more likely to be able to find the problems and repair them than if we just "wing it." By using systems thinking in our classroom plans, we model for our students ways in which they need to plan and monitor their own thinking.

As we plan lessons, a first and last step should be to check to see that we have aligned objectives with the state and local standards, that our lesson plan teaches what is important for students to know and be able to do, and that the assessments that we have planned truly measure success on the objectives. Notice that the student is in the middle of the model provided in Figure 1.1; that is no accident. The written, taught, and assessed curriculum should be student centered; that means that we teach what is best for the student, rather than what is best for politicians, communities, or other adults. What do students need to know and be able to do in order to be successful is at the heart of what we teach. Anytime decisions are made in the classroom or school, the underlying issue should always be, "Is this better for the students?" If the financial decision, the curriculum decision, or the testing decision does not benefit the students, either directly or indirectly, then the decision should be reexamined.

In this book, we will look at the planning steps for a lesson or unit of study based on a model of backward design—beginning with the end in mind. If lesson planning were simply deciding what to tell our students, it would be an easy task; however, planning a lesson involves much more. As teachers we have an obligation to our students to teach them the essential skills, processes, and facts that will help them to be successful now and in the future. Everything that we teach should be research-based and should be taught in such a way that it facilitates meaning and self-reliance. Providing meaning helps students to put the information into long-term memory, and it builds intrinsic motivation. When we provide skills and structures to students that they can use throughout life, we give them self-reliance.

For example, by teaching students to use nonlinguistic organizers, we provide a means to help them learn in any subject and a valuable source for life-long problem solving. Because they are nonlinguistic, these organizers are great tools for English language learners and for students with limited vocabulary skills. Because they are contextual, they are great tools for students from cultures that rely heavily on contextual learning—such as the urban poor.

In *What Every Teacher Should Know About Diverse Learners* and *What Every Teacher Should Know About Student Motivation* (Tileston 2004a, 2004c), I discuss in detail the need for a positive environment and the importance of students acquiring a positive attitude toward classroom tasks. Thus I am not going to discuss these attributes of planning, although I want you to know that they are important to both planning and preplanning. Without the appropriate climate and structures in place, all the planning in the world will not make a difference.

## PREPLANNING TASKS

Before planning a lesson, it is important that you know your students. A teacher can no more plan for a lesson without knowing the strengths and weaknesses of her students than a scientist can examine the effectiveness of a new product on the environment without knowing its strengths and weaknesses.

Look at your student data (i.e., state and national tests, record of attendance, health screening, socioeconomic status, and local testing for special programs). Look for both strengths and weaknesses. If you are unsure about the prerequisite skills that your students bring to your classroom, you can assess them with a pre-test, skills test, discussion questions, or questionnaire to help you plan appropriately. Data should be analyzed for both trends and for gaps. If the data shows that students in your classroom tend to do significantly better in reading than in mathematics, this would be a trend. The trend should be analyzed to find its cause: At what point did the gap occur? Are there gaps in the textbooks and other materials being used in your school? Do teachers in your school have the requisite skills and resources needed to teach mathematics?

Analyze data in regard to various subgroups. The whole group scores may be good, but if any subgroup (e.g., at-risk students, males, females, African Americans, or Hispanics) is not making the same kind of progress as the total group, there is reason to question why. Form 1.1 is a tool a teacher might use to examine data to make decisions about the prerequisite skills of the learners and any gaps in learning.

Once preplanning has been completed, you are ready to plan a lesson that will help students to learn authentically. Authentic learning takes place when students truly know the information and can perform tasks based on that information consistently. Authentic learning is not memorizing material only long enough to be tested and then promptly forgetting it: Authentic learning assures that students understand the material and that they can use it in real-world tasks.

**Form 1.1**    Matrix for Examining Evidence of Prior Learning

| Objective | All Students % mastery | Special Ed. % mastery | Gifted Ed. % mastery | African Am. % mastery | Hispanic % mastery |
|---|---|---|---|---|---|
| 1.1 | | | | | |
| 1.2 | | | | | |
| 1.3 | | | | | |
| 2.1 | | | | | |
| 2.2 | | | | | |
| 2.3 | | | | | |
| 2.4 | | | | | |

## WHAT IS BACKWARD DESIGN?

Wiggins and McTighe (1998) suggest a backward design model for planning that begins not with the lesson, but with our expectations for the end result.

There are three basic steps to designing a lesson using backward design:

1. Identify the desired results.

2. Determine acceptable evidence.

3. Plan learning experiences and instruction.

Before planning the lesson, ask, "What are my expectations for my students?" What do you want the end result of the lesson to be? After teaching the lesson, what do you want students to know in terms of factual knowledge, and what do you want them to be able to do in terms of processes? In other words, what do you want the results to be and how will you know that your students have accomplished what you had hoped they would? According to Wiggins and McTighe (1998),

> We are not free to teach any topic we choose. Rather, we are guided by national, state, district, or institutional standards that specify what students should know and be able to do. These standards provide a framework to help us identify teaching and learning priorities and guide our design of curriculum and assessments. In addition to external standards, we also consider the needs of our students when designing learning experiences. For example, student interests, developmental levels, and previous achievements influence our designs.

Many teachers begin with textbooks, favorite stories, or proven lessons that they have used in the past and plan from that standpoint. A more effective planning strategy, and one that is more likely to get desired results, begins with the desired results. Then the teacher derives what and how she or he will teach based on those desired results and the evidence needed to prove that students understand the information. When we plan using the backward design model, we are less likely that our students will be involved in a "gotcha" when it comes to assessment time.

# 2

# Using Standards as a Guide

*What should students know, understand, and be able to do? What is worthy of understanding? What enduring understandings are desired?*

—G. Wiggins and J. McTighe,
*Understanding by Design*

Some schools provide teachers with a curriculum guide that specifically tells the teacher what must be taught in order to meet the local, state, and national goals. All states now have a set of standards for teaching; some are more specific than others, but they are all helpful in determining what needs to be taught.

In the absence of a curriculum guide, teachers use the state (or national) goals for their subject and grade level to determine what to teach. All learning activities in the classroom should be tied to the state or national goals used by the school. These are usually written in broad terms and in strands. In strands, the information becomes more complex as the student progresses by age.

For example, geometry is taught in grades K–12 but is taught in different ways by age groups and is assessed according to the age of the students. In grades K–2, geometry is taught by introducing students to shapes, such as the square, triangle, and cylinder. Geometry at the high school level uses those same shapes taught at the K–2 level to teach students how to use geometry at a more complex level. Notice that I did not say more difficult level: Learning shapes in K–2 may be just as difficult for those students as learning formulas and plotting segments is for high school students.

Each state includes benchmarks for the goal. Benchmarks indicate the specific knowledge and processes that determine mastery of the goal at a specific grade level. For example, a state goal might be as follows:

Goal 6.3: Students in K–3 will understand how geometry is used in real-world activities.

While this goal is fairly broad in scope, the benchmarks will be narrow. For example,

Benchmark 1: Students will identify a triangle, square, circle, cylinder, and rectangle from objects in the classroom or school building.

Step one, then, in planning for classroom learning, is to identify the state or national goal that will be the basis of the learning.

Step two is to identify the benchmarks that will determine mastery at the given level. Since about 85% of the information tested on state high stakes tests comes from the vocabulary of the benchmark, it is important to isolate the vocabulary in a given benchmark to determine which terms the students will not know. For example, in the benchmark provided above, students would need to know triangle, square, circle, cylinder, and rectangle. They need to know the definitions and the defining characteristics so that they could identify those shapes in other contexts such as objects in a room.

## MAKING CHOICES

With such broad goals as are outlined in state and national standards, how can the classroom teacher make informed choices about what to teach and what to leave out? With a goal written in such broad terms, there are so many options. Wiggins and McTighe (1998) offer a set of questions to help the classroom teacher make decisions about interpreting broad goals and turning them into declarative and procedural objectives.

- *To what extent does the learning have value beyond the classroom?* Another way of saying this is, "Is it relevant to the real world?" A friend of mine who teaches higher-level mathematics keeps a sign in her room promising her students that if she cannot tell them how the math they are working on is used in the real world, then she won't teach it. Sometimes her students challenge her on her promise, but she has remained faithful to show them the real-world application.
- *How critical is the information to understanding and making use of the discipline being studied?* The information being studied should be so meaningful to the discipline that to leave it out would inhibit the students from understanding the underlying ideas of the topic. Wiggins and McTighe (1998) say,

Consider the way professionals work within their chosen disciplines—conducting investigations in science, writing for different purposes (to inform, persuade, or entertain) to real audiences, interpreting events and primary source documents in history, applying mathematics to solve real world problems, researching, critiquing books and movies, and debating issues of social and economic policy.

- *What are the concepts and ideas that provide difficulty for most students to grasp?* What misconceptions do students have about the topic? The National Science Foundation has a wonderful video taken on graduation day at Harvard University in which graduating seniors were asked a series of science questions usually covered in elementary school science. Surprisingly, most of those asked did not know the correct answer. For example, the question was asked, "What causes the seasons of the year?" Most students incorrectly thought that the earth orbiting around the sun caused the seasons. Think about the common mistakes people usually make in understanding your topic and be sure to clear up popular misconceptions your students may have.

- *Is the topic interesting enough to engage students?* Perhaps a better measure would be, "What can we do to make the topic interesting to our students?" Over the years, I have developed a demonstration lesson on the Boston Tea Party. I know that just reading about this event may not hold much excitement for middle school students, so I present them with written invitations to a party when they enter the room. Instead of being made out in the students' names, however, the invitations are addressed in the names of the key players in the incident. Students are placed in groups, each group containing all of the players, and the students then take on roles based on their characters and help others in their group to see their side of the issue. Students love this exercise and remember the learning far better than they would have had I asked them to read the text and answer questions on a worksheet.

Once the classroom teacher has chosen the state goal and the benchmarks for the goal, and then identified the topic or information that will be taught within that goal, the fine points of planning begin.

# 3

# What Do Students Need to Know?

M ost of what is taught in classrooms revolves around declarative information. As a matter of fact, declarative objectives are often referred to as the *what* of the learning, because they are based on facts, dates, names, events, formulas, and vocabulary. There is a difference between teaching students a formula, how and when it is used, and asking students actually to use the formula to solve math problems. When the students are learning about the formula, they are engaged in meeting declarative objectives; when the students are using the formula to solve math problems, they are engaged in meeting procedural objectives. It is important to distinguish between the two types of knowledge, because the ways in which they are taught effectively are different. In most cases, it is also important that students learn the declarative information before being involved in procedural objectives. For example, a teacher would introduce students to the vocabulary involved in the formula and examples of how to use the formula before actually assigning problems for the students to solve.

Once the state goals are identified and the way in which those goals are going to be taught in the classroom, the next major step in planning is to decide which declarative objectives will be important if students are to understand the concepts and vocabulary involved in the subject matter. For example, for the state objective related to shapes that was discussed in Chapter 2, the teacher may have decided to teach a unit on the basic shapes of geometry. The next question that the teacher must ask is, "What do I want my students to know about basic shapes?"

The declarative objectives identified by the teacher are written and displayed in the classroom so that the class has a road map: They know where they are going with the learning (i.e., the state goals) and now they know how they will get there (i.e., through the teacher objectives).

## BUILDING EFFECTIVE DECLARATIVE OBJECTIVES

Declarative objectives are those objectives that define the *what* of learning. They are factual in nature and based around information that we want our students to know. They are not processes but facts—dates, times, vocabulary words, steps, and names. For example, if I were writing declarative objectives for teaching a class based on this book, some of my declarative objectives might look like this:

Participants will know

1. Why planning is important.

2. The definition of *backward design*.

3. The steps in deciding what to teach.

4. The definition of *declarative objectives*.

**Figure 3.1**    Planning for Declarative Objectives

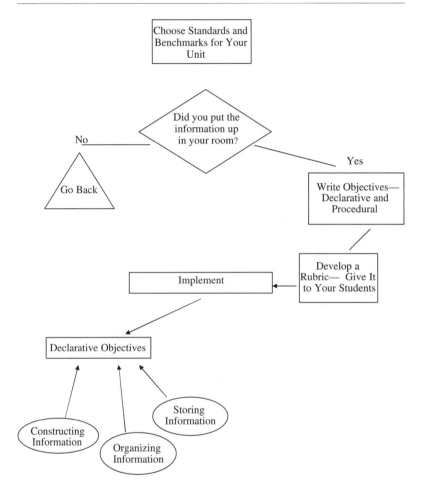

## HELPING STUDENTS REACH SUCCESS WITH DECLARATIVE OBJECTIVES

In order for declarative knowledge to be authentically learned by students, three phases of acquiring the knowledge must take place: constructing meaning, organizing the information for storage, and storing the information for future use. Figure 3.1 is a graphic model of these phases.

The first step for students in mastering declarative objectives is constructing meaning from the information. This is not something that we can do for our students; they must construct the meaning for themselves. However, there are some things that we can do to help facilitate the process.

Second, the students must organize the information in some way to help make meaning and to provide a hook for the brain to remember the information. Declarative information is the hardest type of information for the brain to store and remember; it must have a connector before the brain can process and remember it. We can help our students here by providing the scaffolding necessary for them to create ways to organize information.

Third, students need help to store the information in such a way that they can retrieve it easily and efficiently. The instructional practices that we choose will have a dramatic effect on whether this step takes place.

## AN IN-DEPTH LOOK AT PLANNING THE USE OF DECLARATIVE OBJECTIVES

Let's revisit the three processes involved in helping students to meet declarative objectives for the learning and take a more in-depth look at how the classroom teacher can plan for their success.

### Helping Students Construct Meaning

We help students to construct meaning from the learning by "linking old knowledge with new knowledge, making predictions, verifying them, and filling in a lot of unstated information" (Marzano, 2001). For example, if some of the information in this book is new to you, your brain will have searched your long-term memory to see what you already know about the subject so that the new information can be hooked to the old.

The same is true in the classroom. If you are introducing a lesson on rules in society involving immigration, you cannot assume that your students will know and understand (or even care much) why someone would get in an inner tube and risk his or her life to come to this country or what the risk represents to that person. Students will probably see it as something that happens to others and something they have to study for the test on Friday. In fact, immigration helped to form our democratic society, but that information may not have much of an impact on your students.

A way to hook the information to something they know might be to ask, "What would have to happen in this country to cause you to pick up what you could carry in your arms and go to a country where you knew no one?" By creating a scenario in which your students can be emotionally involved and about which they have strong opinions, you have helped them to hook onto the learning. Now, you can lead them across to the reasons why people immigrate.

Marzano (1998) says, "From a learning perspective, it is impossible to overestimate the importance of using prior knowledge to interpret new information." As a matter of fact, in a meta-analysis study conducted under the auspices of the Mid-continent Regional Education Laboratory in Aurora, Colorado, the teaching strategy of beginning lessons by helping students to link old knowledge to new had a powerful effect on student learning.

Another powerful way that we link old knowledge to new knowledge is by finding out what our students already know about a subject, discussing it, and then moving them to the new knowledge. A KWLH (Know, Want to know, Learned, How I learned) chart is a tool often used for this purpose. Table 3.1 offers an example of a KWLH on immigration.

In this table, the K stands for Know. Have students list five things that they already know about your topic. The W stands for Want to know; ask students to provide three to five things that they would like to know about your topic. There is a danger with older students in asking, "What do you want to know?" They may say, "Nothing." Some teachers have changed this format (depending on the age range of their

**Table 3.1**    KWLH Chart

| Know | Want to Know | Learned | How I Learned |
|------|--------------|---------|---------------|
| Most of us are descendents of immigrants. | Will we run out of land eventually? | Laws related to immigration to this country compared to other countries. | A compare-and-contrast chart. Information taken from text and materials from the Internet. |
| People come into the country illegally. | How can we control illegal entry? | Methods carried out by the border patrols. | Class notes and guest speaker from Immigration Services. |

students) to N or What do you *Need* to Know? Next, the L stands for Learned. This portion is completed at the end of a lesson or unit and is a reflection tool to help students think through what they know at that time that they did not know when they began the lesson or unit. It helps to solidify the information and to put it into long-term memory. Last, the H stands for How I learned. By asking students to identify how they learned the information, we are helping them to understand their own thinking and how learning takes place.

Some other ways that you can help your students construct meaning include the following.

*Pause at intervals in the lesson.* Pause during the lesson, particularly if you are using implicit teaching strategies, and give students an opportunity to talk about the information, think about it, summarize it, do something with it, or ask questions about it. Watch your students' body language to know when they have listened long enough. As a general rule, current brain research suggests that for students 15 years and older, we need to stop every 20 minutes; for students younger than 15, use their age as a guide. In other words, if you are teaching eight-year-olds, stop every 8 minutes. This applies to declarative knowledge only, not procedural knowledge. In procedural knowledge activities, students are doing something with the learning and can attend to the task for much longer periods of time.

*Use the senses.* Engage your students' senses to help them experience the learning. Most of the information coming into the brain comes through the senses. We use auditory learning the most, particularly in secondary schools, but all of the senses play a part in our learning. Use visualization to get students to think about the learning. You might ask your students to imagine what it would be like to have lived during the time of the Declaration of Independence, and guide them through the things they might see. Do the same thing with each of the senses. Tell students that by visualizing what they are learning or trying to do, they help their brain to build connections. A basketball player who can never imagine shooting a free throw may have trouble actually doing it.

## Helping Students Organize Declarative Knowledge

The second step in learning declarative knowledge is helping students to organize the new information. The more we can put information into visual representations, the more we will help our students to construct meaning and to put the information into long-term memory. Jensen (1997) says that at least 87% of the students in the classroom are visual learners—this means that they must see the learning to construct meaning. Visual organizers—sometimes called nonlinguistic organizers, graphic organizers, or advance organizers—help the brain to arrange and make patterns of the information studied. An example of a nonlinguistic organizer used when we are working with anything that requires a description is the *mind map*. To complete a mind map, place the main topic in the center circle, then place attributes or subtopics of that main concept on the spokes coming from the main concept. These can become fairly complicated as ideas are added from the

**Figure 3.2**    Shapes Mind Map

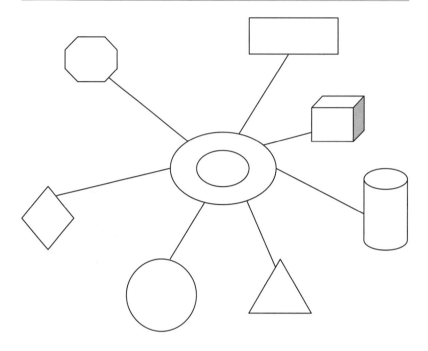

subtopics. Start with simple maps until your students fully understand the concept and then add layers. Figure 3.2 is an example of a simple mind map for the unit on shapes.

Most students are not highly organized, so helping them to organize their notebooks, their notes, and the essential information will be helpful to them and will give them a guide to use in the future. For example, as they set up their notebooks, provide them with some structures—scaffolding—to help them be successful. I have provided an example of a scaffolding tool you might use in a math notebook in Form 3.1.

## Helping Students Store Declarative Knowledge

The third step in learning declarative knowledge is storing the information. I have said that declarative knowledge is the most difficult kind of knowledge for the brain to store: That is

**Form 3.1**    Math Notebook Organizer

| Name of Process | How It Is Expressed | Terms | Definitions/ Examples |
|---|---|---|---|
|  |  |  |  |
|  |  |  |  |

true if declarative information is taught in the traditional method of lecture with drill and practice. There are, however, some tools that can help the brain to store the information in a more acceptable way.

*Use symbols.* You can use symbols to help the brain put the information into categories or patterns. For example, if you are teaching a class that requires a great deal of vocabulary, color-code the vocabulary sheets by the teaching unit in which the vocabulary terms first appeared. If your school cannot afford the colored paper, put a symbol at the top of each vocabulary sheet to help the students keep them straight, or better yet, have the students create their own symbol to help them remember the learning.

When putting students into groups for learning, provide symbols according to their assignment. I like to use frames cut from cardstock paper and laminated. I use a different color for each group. For a lesson on environmental issues, I might give the blue frame to the group that will look at the environment from the standpoint of the new parents, the red frame to the group who will look at the environment from the standpoint of a politician, and the yellow frame for the group that will look at the environment from the standpoint of the factory owner. Sometimes, on those days when students are having trouble recalling information, I need only say, "Remember, it was the information from the red-frame group" and students will remember. I am simply giving the learning a connector to help recall.

*Use movement in the classroom.* The memory system that is attached to movement is very strong, so by combining that memory system with declarative information, we are more likely that students will remember.

*Give the learning a context.* Contextualizing the learning is essential if you are going to reach the urban poor. The culture from which they come transmits information through stories, music, raps, and visual stimuli. If you are going to reach them, you must find ways to teach information in context using names and places and details in a story format. Since most students in the classroom learn better with visuals, the more that we add visual elements to the learning, the more likely it is that more students will be successful.

## In Summary

Declarative objectives are usually taught first, because they contain the facts, vocabulary, dates, times, and so forth that students need in order to carry out procedural objectives. Declarative objectives are stored in the semantic memory system, which is the least efficient of all of the memory systems. That is why our students can't remember all that wonderful information that we have been giving them. The information must make sense to the brain; not only does it need to make sense, but the information should have a personal connection for the learner. By adding music, movement, symbols, and colors to the lesson, we utilize the other memory systems in helping store declarative information and thus provide additional strength to the memory.

# 4

# What Do Students Need to Be Able to Do?

Once students have mastered declarative objectives, it is time to see if they can put that information to use. When we plan for students to use the information, the objectives are *procedural*. Procedural objectives should provide opportunities for students to demonstrate ways to use the declarative knowledge. Declarative objectives should be taught before procedural ones so that students have the resources—both mental and physical—to carry out the tasks.

## DESIGNING PROCEDURAL OBJECTIVES

Procedural objectives are those objectives built around what we want students to be able to do (i.e., to demonstrate through written, oral, kinesthetic, or other means). For example, for a course based on this book, some of my procedural objectives would include the following:

Participants will be able to

1. Design procedural objectives that authentically demonstrate the use of declarative information.

2. Explicitly teach their students to create a variety of mental models.

3. Provide both massed practice and practice over time in sufficient quantity and quality so that students obtain automaticity with the learning.

Just as the successful learning of declarative information involves a series of processes, so learning procedural knowledge involves three parallel but different steps (see Figure 4.1).

First, students need to be able to construct models of the learning mentally and, in some cases, actually. This might be accomplished through imagery, through graphic models, or through student projects.

Second, students need to be able to shape the information so that it becomes their own. Some of the ways that we help students shape the new information is by providing opportunities to practice the learning and by giving them clues about how to make the process work smoothly.

Third, students must internalize procedural knowledge through practice over time. We help students internalize and give the information automaticity by providing adequate opportunities for them to work with the process and by providing feedback often.

Let's look at these important factors that must be incorporated in using procedural objectives effectively.

## CONSTRUCTING MENTAL MODELS

Just as the first phase of learning a skill or process is developing a rough model of the steps involved, so learning procedural knowledge is a matter of learning and understanding the steps involved in demonstrating the process. Some ways to do this include:

**Figure 4.1** Planning for Procedural Objectives

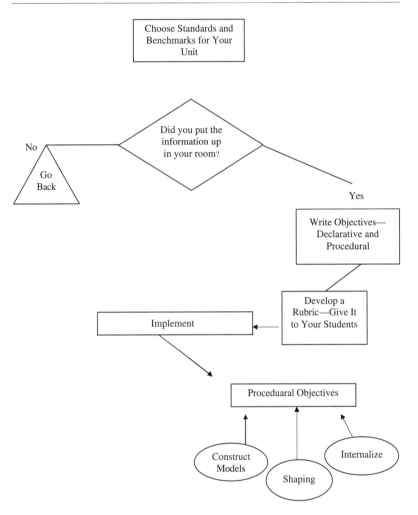

- Teaching students to talk through the process by demonstrating how you talk yourself through new learning. For example, a French teacher might think aloud as she goes through the process of breaking a sentence into its grammatical parts.
- Providing a written set of steps. For example, a teacher provides students with the written steps for writing a

limerick and then demonstrates each step as she reads a limerick.

- Providing models or examples for students. For the unit of study on shapes, the teacher might bring models of squares, rectangles, and cylinders for students to hold and examine.
- Teaching students to use flow charts or other visual models. For example, for a unit on weather, the teacher might have the students work in small groups to make a flow chart of the steps that take place in a weather pattern.
- Teaching students to mentally rehearse the steps involved in a process. For example, a physical education teacher might ask students to rehearse the process of shooting a basket before they actually try it with a basketball.
- Connecting the new skill to a skill they already know how to do.

## SHAPING THE INFORMATION

Wiggins and McTighe (1998) write that "constructing an initial mental model for a new skill or process is just the first step in learning procedural knowledge":

> Once we actually begin to use the skill or process, we usually alter our initial model. As we start to find out what works and what doesn't work, we modify our approach, adding some things and dropping others. This is called shaping. For example, after constructing an initial model for performing long division, we may begin to discover some shortcuts and tricks that make the process work better for us.

Some ways that we help students shape the procedural knowledge include the following:

- Demonstrating and providing practice in the skill or process. As the teacher, you must provide general rules or heuristics in how to do a new process and then provide adequate opportunities for students to practice the learning before you assess.
- Pointing out possible pitfalls or common errors that people make when executing the process. For example, a teacher showing students the steps involved in reading a contour map tells them that it is easy to misinterpret the altitudes for each contour layer and to make incorrect assumptions about specific types of contours.
- Providing a variety of situations in which students can use a specific skill or process. Wiggins and McTighe (1998) offer the example of a writing teacher who "demonstrates how she changes the decisions she makes during the editing process based on the audience for whom her writing is intended. She then has students edit a single essay for two different audiences and compare the results."

## FACILITATING AUTOMATICITY

The last aspect of learning a new skill or process is doing something to the point that you can do it without conscious thought. This is referred to as *automaticity*. Here are some guidelines to help you help your students attain automaticity:

- Provide adequate opportunities for practice. Help students self-assess the amount of practice they need and their speed and accuracy.
- Have students keep a chart of their progress and to self-assess their work.
- Provide opportunities for metacognition or reflection.
- Provide students with a rubric with which they can self-assess their work. A rubric provides descriptors for each level of performance. Table 4.1 is an example of a

**Table 4.1**    Rubric for Planning Procedural Objectives

| Expert Level | Proficient Level | Emerging Level | Beginning Level |
|---|---|---|---|
| Procedural objectives are written so that they clearly state what it is that we want the students to be able to do with the declarative knowledge. The objectives employ a wide variety of techniques, including oral, visual, and kinesthetic modalities. | Procedural objectives are written so that they clearly state what it is that we want the students to be able to do with the declarative knowledge. The objectives employ at least two of the three common modalities of learning. | Procedural objectives are written so that they clearly state what it is that we want the students to be able to do with the declarative knowledge. The objectives employ at least the visual modality of learning. | Procedural objectives are written so that they clearly state what it is that we want the students to be able to do with the declarative knowledge. The objectives are limited in scope. |
| Students are given adequate time to practice the learning before being assessed. There is evidence that practice has been massed and that it has been spread over time. | Students are given adequate time to practice the learning before being assessed. There is evidence that practice has been massed and that it has been spread over time. | Students are given adequate time to practice the learning before being assessed. There is evidence that practice has been massed and that it has been spread over time. | Students are given adequate time to practice the learning before being assessed. Practice has either been massed or spread over time, but not both. |
| All students show automaticity. Provisions have been made for those students who need additional practice. | Most students show automaticity. Provisions have been made for those students who need additional practice. | Only the faster learners in the classroom show automaticity. Provisions have been made for those students who need additional practice. | Many of the students do not show automaticity. Provisions have not been made for those students who need additional practice. |

*(Continued)*

**Table 4.1** Continued

| Expert Level | Proficient Level | Emerging Level | Beginning Level |
|---|---|---|---|
| Students have received explicit instruction on how to develop mental models. The teacher has modeled how he or she uses positive self-talk when working with new information. | Students have received explicit instruction on how to develop mental models. The teacher has modeled how he or she uses positive self-talk when working with new information. | Students have received explicit instruction on how to develop mental models. The teacher has modeled how he or she uses positive self-talk when working with new information. | Students have received little or no instruction on how to develop mental models. The teacher has limited input into modeling positive self-talk. |
| There is evidence that students have been taught how to use visualization to picture themselves doing an activity and to picture the steps that need to be taken to be successful. | There is evidence that students have been taught how to use visualization to picture themselves doing an activity and to picture the steps that need to be taken to be successful. | The teacher has only used visualization in a limited capacity for some tasks. | Visualization has not been used in the classroom. |
| There is a direct and specific alignment between the procedural objectives, the rubric for grading, and the information provided to the students. | Alignment between the procedural objectives, the rubric for grading, and the information provided to students shows thought and contains only minor gaps. | Alignment between the procedural objectives, the rubric for grading, and the information provided to students shows specific gaps. | Alignment between the procedural objectives, the rubric for grading, and the information provided to students is greatly limited or nonexistent. |

rubric that might be used for determining whether procedural objectives are adequately planned and executed in the classroom.

## In Summary

Through this chapter we have examined procedural objectives in terms of what they are and how they should be written. We have also moved through a process to ensure that procedural objectives are adequately taught to students and that students are able to perform these objectives with the end result of automaticity.

I modeled this process by providing procedural objectives for the chapter, teaching the information, and then creating a rubric that shows explicitly how the objectives, the information, and the rubric are connected. Although I provided this information for procedural objectives only, all lessons should include both the declarative and procedural objectives in this format.

# 5

# Where Is the Evidence of Learning?

If we want students to learn at a quality level and to produce products that reflect that quality, students need to know our expectations and how they will be assessed. There was a time when I would ask my students to do their work at a quality level, only to find that my definition of *quality* and their definition were not necessarily the same. I no longer leave this to chance.

Before we ever plan the learning experiences and instruction, we need to use a visual representation that tells students exactly what we expect and how we will grade their work based on those expectations. Many teachers use a matrix or rubric as their visual representation (see Tileston, 2004b, for different assessment instruments and information about building rubrics). Look back at the Table 4.1 in Chapter 4: It is a rubric based on four criteria and four levels of performance. Rubrics can be based on fewer or more criteria and levels of performance. Table 5.1 is an example of a simple rubric for an elementary math assignment

**Table 5.1**    Performance Standards Rubric

| Level | Standard to Be Achieved |
| --- | --- |
| 4. Mathematician | Understands the math concept as indicated by an ability to use the concept in context and to explain the concept. |
| 3. Arriving | Understands the basics of the math concept as indicated by an ability to use the concept, although some details may be missing. |
| 2. Emerging | Has some basic understanding of the concept, but is not able to effectively communicate either in written or spoken language. |
| 1. Beginning | Work is either not completed or completed with evidence that the student neither understands the concept nor is able to articulate the concept either visually or orally. |

*Rubric*
*Website*

If you are unsure about creating rubrics for your classroom, the Website www.therubricator.com provides opportunities for you to practice setting up simple to more complex rubrics.

## How Will We Know That Students Understand?

"How will we know if students have achieved the desired results and met the standards? What will we accept as evidence of student understanding and proficiency?" ask Wiggins and McTighe (1998). Their answer is that the backward design approach "encourages us to think about a unit or course in terms of the collected assessment evidence needed to document and validate that the desired learning has been achieved, so that the course is not just content to be covered or a series of learning activities."

As you teach a lesson or unit, what benchmarks are you using to measure student learning? When the benchmark step is eliminated, teachers may teach the content only to find at the end of the unit that the students have a minimal understanding of the lessons. It is much more difficult to go back and re-teach at this point. Assessment of the learning should be ongoing, and it should include many methods of evaluation. The evaluation of procedural knowledge will differ from the evaluation of declarative knowledge. The evaluation should match the rubric given to students at the beginning of the unit of study or lesson.

Following are some ways to determine acceptable evidence that students know and understand.

## Informal Checks for Understanding

*Hand Signals.* Ask students to provide hand signals to indicate the level of understanding. For example, ask them to give a thumbs-up if they understand and can explain it, to give a thumbs-down if they do not yet understand, and to wave their hands if not completely sure that they understand. A variation of this technique is to ask students to tell you on a scale of 1 to 3 their understanding of a concept, with 1 being *not at all* and 3 being *completely.*

*Question Box.* Provide a place in your room for students to ask questions, such as a question box in which students place questions.

*Ticket Out the Door.* A technique I like is "Ticket Out the Door." I provide students with a prompt, such as, "Name one thing that you learned today and one thing that you still do not understand. This will be your ticket out the door when the bell rings." Sometimes I vary this by saying, "Tell me one way you could use the math that you learned today." For young children or any students with a limited vocabulary, pictures with facial expressions could be used. Figure 5.1 is an example

**Figure 5.1**    Using Pictures to Evaluate the Learning

of how students might show how they feel about the learning using expressions.

*Asking Questions.* Asking questions is another way to informally find out if students understand the new information. Asking the right questions involves not only posing the question in the right format, but also doing so in such a way that students do not feel threatened. Students need to believe that it is okay to be a risk taker. Try to create an atmosphere in your classroom that says it is okay to be wrong, but that it is not okay to not try at all. This also means that you must create an atmosphere that says, "We do not laugh at others' mistakes; there an absolutely no put-downs in this class."

One of the difficulties that new teachers face is how to ask questions so that students do not rely on a simple "yes" or "no" answer. The following question stems, from Wiggins and McTighe (1998), are good models:

How is . . . similar to/different from . . . ?

What are the characteristics or parts of . . . ?

In what other ways might we show or illustrate . . . ?

What is the big idea/key concept/moral in . . . ?

How does . . . relate to . . . ?

What ideas or details can you add to . . . ?

Give an example of . . . .

What is wrong with . . . ?

What might you infer from . . . ?

What conclusions might be drawn from . . . ?

What question are we trying to answer? What problem are we trying to solve?

What are you assuming about . . . ?

What might happen if . . . ?

What criteria would you use to judge or evaluate . . . ?

What evidence supports . . . ?

How might we prove/confirm . . . ?

How might this be viewed from the perspective of . . . ?

What alternatives should be considered?

Help students learn to ask good questions as well by using a tool such as "Fat and Skinny Questions." Skinny questions are those that can be answered with simple answers, such as "yes" or "no"; fat questions require more thought, may not have one answer, and call for more than a one- or two-word answer (see Form 5.1). This is a great tool to get good questioning strategies going.

## Ask Students to Summarize the Learning

One of the best strategies that we use with our students is to provide opportunities for them to process the new information. There are a great many tools that allow the teacher to involve students in this technique. One that I like to use is called PMI (Positive–Minus–Interesting; see Form 5.2). For a PMI, ask students to write something positive—to write about what they liked in the lesson or what they learned that they did not know when they began. Then, ask students to list

**Form 5.1**    Learning to Formulate Fat and Skinny Questions

| *Skinny Questions* | *Fat Questions* |
| --- | --- |
| Who? | How? |
| What? | Why? |
| When? | What do you think? |
| Where? | Explain |

something negative—what they still do not understand, what bothered them about the lesson, what was not clear to them, or what they disagreed with, Finally, ask students to add to the learning with interesting observations or ideas that they had during the learning.

## Learning Logs

Learning logs are a great tool for helping students to summarize information and to provide their own insights into the learning. In a learning log, students are usually given a prompt and then asked to write their own thoughts. For example, for a unit on immigration, a beginning prompt might be to ask students what kinds of things would cause them to leave this country for another or to ask what would have to happen on the medical or political front to make them leave.

I like to use this tool at the end of a lesson as well. For the unit on shapes, I might ask students to tell me what they learned about shapes that they did not know before the lesson, or I might ask a "what if" question, such as, "What if everything in the world was round?" I also like interactive logs in

**Form 5.2**    PMI Chart

| Positive (What did you learn?) | Minus (What questions were not answered?) | Interesting (What can you add to the learning?) |
|---|---|---|
|  |  |  |
|  |  |  |
|  |  |  |

which I provide information from the text or other materials on the left side and students then write their comments on the right side. Sometimes, I give them a prompt, such as, "What can you infer from the paragraph?" or "What would you have done?" Form 5.3 is an example of a learning log that I use to demonstrate this technique.

Other ways that the teacher might determine if students understand the information is through observation or through dialogue with the students. Of course, a pencil-and-paper test is also a way to determine if students understand.

## How Will We Know That Students Can Use the Information?

One of the best ways that we can be sure that students can use the information is to provide opportunities for them to demonstrate this ability. Performance tasks and projects provide a great

**Form 5.3**    Learning Log

| *Essay on Jealousy* | Log |
|---|---|

*Essay on Jealousy*

The theme of jealousy is not a new one. Since the beginning of time, jealousy has caused friction in families, disorder, wars, assault, and divisions in relationships. Was it not jealousy that caused the division between the first brothers, Cain and Abel? Is it not jealousy that causes the breakup of many relationships? Jealousy has helped us to coin such phrases as "green-eyed monster" and "green with envy." There is even a Website for songs of jealousy. The basic motive behind jealousy has been a subject for controversy over the ages. What *is* jealousy?

**Is it fear?** Some dictionaries will say that the motive of jealousy is fear. We are afraid that someone else will excel and we will not. We are afraid that our partner will find someone else more appealing and we will be left alone. We fear that we will never be successful, have money, be beautiful, or attain some other measure of success deemed important to us.

**Is it envy?** Most often, envy is used synonymously with jealousy. We envy what someone else has or has accomplished. We envy what we do not have. We envy the good fortune of our neighbors, and we fear that our own value has been lessened by their good fortune. What do we have that we can talk about when our neighbors, friends, siblings, or significant others bring us the news of their great achievements or acquisitions?

**Is it both?** The best way to understand jealousy is to ask ourselves what triggers jealousy in us. Are we afraid that we will not be able to measure up to what others are doing? Do I genuinely dislike another because they have what I do not? Is my fear rational, because their good fortune will lead to my demise, my loss of status, or loss of my job? Will another's gain indeed be my loss? Or is it that I do not begrudge my neighbor his good fortune; I just wish the same would happen to me?

avenue for assessing procedural objectives. Some characteristics of performance tasks and projects include the following:

- They should mimic real-world projects. For example, students studying weather patterns might plot the major earthquakes of the world in terms of time of day, duration, magnitude, amount of damage, and number of lives lost. Students may then look for trends in the data. This is a real-world project, because there are scientists who do this same work.
- Performance tasks typically require the student to address a specific audience.
- They allow the student greater opportunity to personalize the task, because they include choices to be made by the student.
- The task, criteria, and standards are known in advance, usually through a rubric or matrix provided by the teacher so there are no surprises.

# 6

# How Do We Plan Meaningful Learning Experiences?

Once declarative and procedural objectives based on state standards have been written, a rubric has been drawn, and expectations for the learning have been set, the next point of the alignment triangle must be attended to. This part of the alignment process deals with planning learning experiences that will cause students to meet the objectives. Without appropriate planning for these activities, they have little likelihood of occurring.

We live in an age of great advances in neural science. Those advances have helped us to know some of the tools that work well with students and some that don't work quite so well. As we plan for student learning and for our students to become self-directed learners, it is important to look at three facets of brain research that show us what is necessary for quality learning.

## INSTRUCTIONAL STRATEGIES TO HELP STUDENTS LEARN DECLARATIVE KNOWLEDGE

In Chapter 3, declarative knowledge was broken down into three important steps that must take place before students can effectively learn information: constructing meaning, organizing information, and storing information.

### Building Connections Between Old Learning and New Learning

The first step is for students to construct meaning from the declarative information. One of the most powerful ways that we can help students do this is by helping them to connect what they already know to the new information.

Prior to introducing a new lesson, students will pay attention and learn better if attention is given to the *anticipation of meaning*. This is the same tactic often used by the news media: Before the newscast, a newscaster will appear on the television screen to say something like, "Major breakthrough in the XYZ affair—stay tuned." Using strategies that draw the student into the learning is one way to do that. The brain likes patterns and looks for connections to prior experiences and prior knowledge. When we introduce new material to our students, there are a few moments of panic as the brain searches for what it already knows or has experienced with which it can connect the new information.

Emotion and relevance are key factors to gaining student attention and motivation. Use them to help students hook onto the new learning. I call this *personal connection*, because we are literally setting up a personal reason for learning. The personal connection is

- The process of going from the known to the unknown
- The piece that gives meaning to the learning process

- The link between old knowledge and new knowledge
- The bridge between disciplines
- The hook that pulls the students into the lesson

Throughout this book, I have provided examples of ways that teachers can help students connect old knowledge to new knowledge. The KWLH tool discussed in Chapter 4 and the learning log used for the lesson on immigration are samples tools. Other ways to help students make connections include the following strategies.

*We'd Rather.* "We'd Rather" is a tool used to build empathy when students may not have had a prior experience with which to compare to the new learning. For example, in elementary school, before teaching a lesson on weather, we might read John Bianchi's *Snowed In at Pokeweed Public School* and *Spring Break at Pokeweed Public School* to compare and contrast the weather conditions. I would not assume that my students would know what it is like to be snowed in somewhere. I might use the tool "We'd Rather" to help build empathy for the students snowed in overnight at school. For this activity, I give the students pictures of various activities in which they could get involved in the story. Some of the examples are actual activities from the book; others are not. I ask students to choose three things they would do if they were snowed in at school overnight, such as play games, paint or draw pictures, and play in the snow.

At the secondary level, I use this technique when I teach the short story "After Twenty Years", by O'Henry. In this short story, two high school seniors make a pact to meet in the same place 20 years later. Twenty years pass and the young men meet again: one of the young men is a police officer; the law wants the other man. Again, I build empathy for the characters by asking my students what they would be willing to do for their jobs. I give them several choices, including "Do my job, no matter what the cost." I have hooked my students into the lesson from the very beginning, because they want to see

**Form 6.1**    Find Someone Who . . .

*Directions:* For each of the questions below, find a different person who can provide an answer. Ask each person who answers a question to sign his or her name by the question that he or she answered.

Find someone who . . .

1. Owns a pair of snowshoes.

2. Can sing *Frosty the Snowman.*

3. Knows how to ice skate.

4. Knows the freezing temperature of water.

5. Has lived in a state where it snows often.

6. Knows how to use a camera.

7. Has been in a snowstorm.

8. Has seen a photograph of a snowflake.

what the characters in the story choose to do. I have given the learning a personal connection where one does not naturally exist.

*Find Someone Who. . . .* This is a great tool to build interest in the learning at the beginning of a lesson. When I teach a demonstration lesson on *Snowflake Bentley,* the true story of the man who first photographed snowflakes and determined that each flake is different, I use this tool. Form 6.1 is an elementary example for *Snowflake Bentley.*

## Organizing/Planning Tools

The second step for students learning declarative information is to organize the information. Anytime we put information into categories, organizers, or chunks, we help our students to learn more efficiently and at a faster rate. Students do not come to us naturally organized, so organizing/planning skills should be a part of what we teach to our students. Here are a few examples of tools that help students to organize their information.

*Chapter Frame.* A chapter frame might be used to help students organize the main ideas of a lesson and to help them recall declarative information. This tool is an example of a linguistic organizer. Because the organizer gives context to the learning, it helps students to store the information in long-term memory more efficiently. Declarative information is easier to store when it has a context or hook. Form 6.2 provides a sample story frame.

*Story Map.* A story map is similar to a chapter frame, except students place the information from a single story or book into a frame (see Form 6.3).

*Nonlinguistic Organizers.* Nonlinguistic organizers are great tools for helping students give structure to the learning. Because more than 87% of the students in any given classroom are visual learners, using these organizers helps assure that these learners truly understand the information being provided. These organizers tend to follow patterns based on their purpose. Some of the patterns identified by Marzano (1992) include

- Descriptive patterns, which are used to organize facts or characteristics about specific persons, places, things, and events. The facts or characteristics need be in no particular order. The mind map tool is an example of this type of pattern.

*(Text continues on page 48)*

**Form 6.2**    Chapter Frame

Chapter _____ takes place _____

_____

_____

_____.

_____ is an important character and can be described as

_____

_____

_____.

Another character is _____ and can be described as

_____

_____

_____.

In this chapter, the action starts when _____

_____

_____

_____.

After that, _____ and

_____

_____

_____.

The chapter ends with _____

_____

_____

_____.

**Form 6.3**    Story Map

The Setting:

Characters:

---

The Problem:

---

The Goal

---

Event 1

---

Event 2

---

Event 3

---

Event 4

---

Event 5

---

Event 6

**Figure 6.1**    Process/Cause Patterns

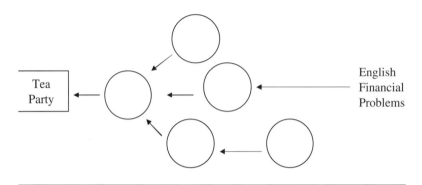

- Sequence patterns, which are used to organize events in a specific chronological order. Timelines are an example of this pattern.
- Process/cause patterns, which are used to organize information into a causal network leading to a specific outcome or into a sequence of steps leading to a specific product. A teacher might use this pattern when we know the end result but we want to analyze how it occurred. For example, the events leading to the Boston Tea Party would certainly include such things as financial problems in England, the issue of taxation without representation, and the Stamp Act. A nonlinguistic representation might take on a pattern, such as the one shown in Figure 6.1.
- Branching patterns, which show the parts of systems, classes and subclasses, and hierarchical relationships (Parks & Black, 1992). For a study of parts of speech, a branching diagram might look something like the diagram in Figure 6.2.

## Storing Declarative Information

Information in long-term memory is stored in memory pathways that correlate to the type of information being stored and the way that it was learned. Some pathways are more efficient than others. Unfortunately, the memory

**Figure 6.2.**    Branching Diagram

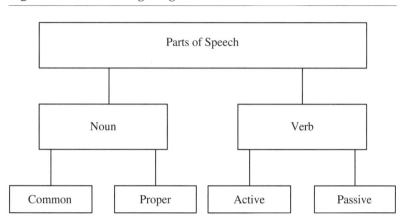

pathway in which most declarative information is stored—the semantic memory—is the least efficient of the various memory pathways. This explains, in part, why our students have so much difficulty remembering all that wonderful information that we give to them.

In order for the semantic memory system to store and retrieve declarative information, it must have a connector. As Sprenger (2002) says,

> Important information in the form of facts must be cataloged through the hippocampus if it is to be held in long-term memory. The difficulty lies in the fact that the information has to go to working memory first. Working memory is a process in which information is held in the prefrontal cortex. Here, it is rehearsed, elaborated on, and worked with until it can be stored in long-term memory.

We help students store declarative information by giving the information a context and by providing structures to help students recall the information. For example, color-coding vocabulary sheets according to the topic helps students sort the information into a pattern that is compatible for the brain. Using symbols, such as frames (signifying frames of reference), when discussing information from different viewpoints helps sort the information for storage. Adding movement to the learning will also help the brain to store the information in a format that makes recall easier.

One powerful method of helping students to store information that has emerged through brain research is to give students time to reflect on the learning. Reflecting on the learning helps students make meaning and put information into long-term memory. Students need the opportunity to reflect on their learning and on the way in which they learn. Student journals are a form of learning log that are often used in classrooms. Below are questions that might be used as prompts to help students write:

- "What I really understood today was . . ."
- "I've changed my mind about . . ."
- "A new insight or discovery for me was . . ."
- "The one thing I'll remember is . . ."
- "I'm really confused about . . ."
- "These are some questions I have . . ."
- "Something I'd like to know more about is . . ."
- "What I am finding hardest right now is . . ."
- "What mistakes did I make and why?"
- "What I liked best was . . ."
- "How am I feeling about [math, science, etc.]?"

Using journal writing to help students explore connections between new and previously learned information might include such questions as

- "How does what I learned today fit with what I already know?"
- "How is this process similar to one I have learned before?"

Using journals to help students analyze problems in math might include questions like the following:

- "What problem was most difficult for me? Why?"
- "How did I try to solve the problem?"
- "Which problem did I like best? Why?"
- "What are the steps I used to solve a problem?"

## INSTRUCTIONAL STRATEGIES TO HELP STUDENTS LEARN PROCEDURAL KNOWLEDGE

In Chapter 4, the three phases necessary for learning procedural knowledge were discussed: constructing models, shaping information, and internalizing procedures. Let's revisit these phases in regard to how we can help students to be successful in engaging procedural objectives.

### Constructing Models

Marzano (1992) says that, before we can construct models for our students, we must first understand the three basic types of strategies that are used to do this. They are algorithms, tactics, and strategies.

Algorithms involve specific steps that give definite results every time they are carried out (Anderson, 1990). Marzano (1992) uses the example of doing multiplication: If a student follows the step-by-step process for multiplication, he or she should get the same results each time the task is performed. If a student does not get the correct answer, he or she did not follow the step-by-step algorithm provided for the task.

Tactics, according to Snowman and McCown (1984), help students accomplish their goals, but don't necessarily provide the same end result every time. This is because tactics involve general rules rather than a step-by-step process. Marzano (1992) uses the example of reading a bar graph. There are general rules involved in reading a bar graph, but those rules do not give the same results every time. The probability of success is there, but there is not the assurance that the student has with algorithms.

Strategies are more general in nature than algorithms and tactics, because they are not specific to any given task.

Strategies provide a way to approach a task and vary with the user. All three of these models are important in helping students to gain success in learning procedural knowledge. Marzano (1992) lists two powerful ways to help students construct knowledge.

*1. Using Self-Talk to Walk Through a Process.* Students need to observe the teacher using positive self-talk to work through a process so that they can use that same method as they work through problems and processes themselves. For example, a teacher might write a sentence on the board that contains a word unfamiliar to the students. The teacher would talk about the process that he or she goes through in deciding how to pronounce the word. Self-talk is a valuable tool to teach to our students, because it will be very helpful as they work through procedures where there are problems. Students who do not know how to monitor and adjust for problems will more likely throw up their hands and quit. Teaching them to use self-talk to walk through problems helps limit impulsivity.

*2. Using Flow Charts to Build Structure in the Learning.* One of the most difficult forms of writing for my students is describing a process. For example, if I were to give my students the writing stem, "Describe how you would tell someone the steps needed in brushing your teeth," many of my students would struggle. However, if I teach my students to use a flow chart first to organize their ideas, the writing becomes a much easier task. Flow charts are a way for students to see the information before they put it into written form. The information might involve how to solve a math problem, the steps leading to an event in history, the processes that take place in a science experiment, or the steps involved in writing a theme. In Chapter 1, I provided a flow chart on the steps necessary for planning.

Of course, specifically teaching students the tactics, algorithms, and strategies used in procedural knowledge is valuable not just for the classroom, but for life.

## Shaping Procedural Knowledge

It is during the critical phase of shaping information that students take the processes learned through tactics, algorithms, and strategies and make them their own. That is, they learn by practicing the learning. This is the guided practice phase of the lesson. During this time, students are learning on a first-hand basis whether the strategy they selected for demonstrating the knowledge will work and, if not, what needs to be done to see that they find success. The shaping process should provide adequate time and feedback so that students know that they know.

## Internalizing Procedural Knowledge (Automaticity)

Automaticity is achieved when students practice a process sufficiently so that they can perform the task with accuracy and consistency. Practice may be massed—that is, practiced over and over in a concentrated period of time—and it may be practiced over a long period of time in a spiral fashion. Richard Bandler (1988) says that, in order for a learner to be convinced of what he or she knows, three criteria must be met.

First, the learner must have the information reinforced in the modality—visual, auditory, or kinesthetic—most comfortable for the learner. According to Jensen (1997), visual learners may need to see a visual representation of the learning before believing it; auditory learners may need to discuss the information before they believe they know the information; and kinesthetic learners may need to see and touch a model before they believe that they have learned.

Second, the information must be reinforced the right number of times. The number of times varies with the learner and with the information.

Third, the information must be reinforced for a sufficient length of time. Again, the length of time may be minutes to hours depending on the learner and the information being learned.

## What Is Understanding?

Wiggins and McTighe (1998) offer six facets that can be used to determine if students truly understand the learning. They say that students who understand can

1. *Explain*—this includes such things as the ability to tell the information in the student's own words and to be able to teach the concept to someone else. Students who can explain also understand the big picture, and they understand and avoid common misunderstandings about the learning.

2. *Interpret*—this includes the ability to read between the lines and to understand the purpose and meaning of the information.

3. *Apply*—the student can use the information in a way that is meaningful to him- or herself and to others.

4. *See in perspective*—this means that the student knows the importance of the information, the background, and the limits of the information.

5. *Demonstrate empathy*—students who have this attribute can project themselves into the situations discussed. For example, for the lesson on immigration, when students discuss what would make them leave this country and then related their reasons to the common reasons that people actually immigrate, they demonstrate empathy.

6. *Reveal self-knowledge*—this means that the student can self-assess and can use metacognition effectively. For instance, a student who possessed self-knowledge would accurately use the PMI or KWLH tools discussed throughout this book.

# 7

# Putting Planning Into Practice

C hapter 1 began by explaining that, when planning lessons, the teacher begins with the end in mind. Through the succeeding chapters, we've come to see the order and way in which we plan lessons and the way we teach them have a direct effect on whether students are teacher-directed or self-directed. We know that the teacher who simply stands in front of a class spewing information for the students to memorize for the test on Friday has little impact on learning, either now or in the future. Each of us must make meaning of the information for it to have lasting impact; meaning making is something that the students must do for themselves.

In this chapter, we will look at what a lesson plan built around this model of planning might look like.

## ELEMENTARY LESSON ON PLANNING (GRADE 2 UNIT)

For an elementary lesson on setting goals and planning, the state standard might look something like this:

Standard: Sets and manages goals

Benchmarks:
- K–3 Identifies resources necessary to complete a goal
- K–3 Displays a sense of personal direction and purpose
- K–3 Maintains an awareness of proximity to goal
- K–3 Makes contingency plans

Using the state standards and benchmarks as a guide, I, as teacher, might develop objectives for the classroom content. Objectives show our expectations for our students' learning. A declarative objective indicates the factual information that students will know as a result of the lesson or lessons; a procedural objective indicates what students will be able to do with the factual knowledge. For a lesson on planning for Grade 2, my objectives might be written like this:

Declarative Objectives: Students will know
- The vocabulary related to planning
- The steps of planning
- How planning is used in the real world
- Why planning is important

Procedural Objectives: Students will be able to
- Identify and use the vocabulary related to planning
- Create and implement a plan for a given task
- Plan for problems in implementation
- Evaluate personal plans

The next step in planning is to create a rubric for how I will assess the learning (see Table 7.1). In order to do that, I will look back at the declarative and procedural objectives and ask, "How will I be assured that the students know the information, and how will I know that they can use the information meaningfully?" The rubric should tie directly to my objectives. As I create the rubric, I must ask what the critical areas for assessment will be. For this unit, I chose four areas to assess:

- Knowing the terminology associated with the unit
- Being able to effectively use the information in the procedures assigned
- Being able to explain what students know and to self-evaluate their work
- Being able to follow through with planning

Next, as I decide how I will deliver the information in the classroom, I look at the declarative and procedural objectives in regard to what must be done in order not only to make the information meaningful, but also to assure that students put the information into long-term memory.

**Table 7.1**    Rubric for Assessing Student Learning

| Advanced planner | Emerging planner | Beginning planner |
|---|---|---|
| Knows terms associated with planning and can predict possible problems accurately. | Knows terms associated with planning and can make limited predictions about the possible problems. | Shallow level of understanding of the terms. Is not able to predict problems accurately. |
| Demonstrates advanced ability to plan for a given task and to carry out that plan. | Demonstrates ability to construct a plan for a given task and to carry out that plan. | Limited ability to construct a plan without help from the teacher. |
| Participates in all activities with enthusiasm and is able to discuss the learning on an in-depth level. | Participates in all activities with some encouragement and is able to discuss the learning on a limited basis. | Participates in all activities and is able to join in discussions on a limited basis. |

Let's look at the declarative knowledge first. Declarative knowledge represents the factual knowledge that students will know and understand by the end of the unit. Which instructional practices will help ensure that my students learn and truly understand the declarative knowledge? There are three mental processes that help facilitate declarative knowledge: meaning making, organizing information, and storing information in ways that make retrieval more efficient. Let's examine these and determine how they might be effectively carried out in this lesson.

The first process in learning declarative information is often called *meaning making*. It is in this phase that the new information must make sense to the student personally. The single most important thing that we can do to create meaning for the learner is to use prior knowledge and the experiences of the students to introduce the new knowledge. This is important because it follows the way our brain works. The brain seeks patterns naturally. Anytime we throw out new information to our students, there are a few moments while their brains are searching to see what they already know or have experienced to help the brain make sense of the new information. For the lesson on planning, I might ask my students if they have ever taken a trip, made a cake, or planned a party. Then I might ask, "What did you do to plan? Did it work out well? What materials did you need? Did you forget something? Would a written plan have helped you remember?" I am specifically taking the context of something they have done or experienced and giving personal meaning to the new learning.

The second phase of processing declarative knowledge is organizing the information. We organize the information in two ways: by identifying what is important and what is not, and by creating either a linguistic or nonlinguistic model for the information. To help my students understand what a plan is and what it is not, I might point out the events cited by my students (i.e., baking a cake, planning a party, or taking a trip) as either having a plan or not, based on the information provided by the students. A plan has sequential parts, whereas a non-plan is not sequential and not well though out—which is why things may go wrong.

To provide opportunities for my students to organize information into linguistic and/or nonlinguistic formats, I will directly teach them how to create both types of organizers. Linguistic organizers are structures that use words to convey meaning. For example, an outline, journal writing, and summarizing are linguistic models. A nonlinguistic model relies on structure, symbols, and graphics to convey meaning. Examples of nonlinguistic organizers include mind maps, circle maps, and timelines.

The third phase of learning declarative knowledge is storing the information so that it can be easily retrieved when needed. As a teacher, I can deliver wonderful lessons, but if my students do not store and retrieve the information, it has been for nothing. How we store the information is determined by how we rehearse the new learning. Rehearsal can be rote or elaborative. Rote rehearsal involves saying, reading, or writing the information a sufficient number of times so that it is remembered. We learn math formulas, the names of states, and spelling words this way. Anything that is best learned in the context in which it is presented can be learned with rote rehearsal. The key is the amount of rehearsal and whether the information is revisited often enough so that students remember the learning.

A more efficient way to rehearse information is through elaborative rehearsal. Elaborative rehearsal is necessary if we want students to be able to use the information in other contexts. For example, students should be able to use the vocabulary words related to planning in other contexts, so I would not teach those words with rote rehearsal but rather with elaborative methods. Some elaborative methods include simulations, nonlinguistic organizers, and imagery.

## LESSON ONE: PLANNING STEPS

Planning instructional strategies for declarative objectives might look something like this:

Standard: Sets and manages goals

Benchmarks: Identifies resources necessary to complete a goal
- Displays a sense of personal direction and purpose
- Maintains an awareness of proximity to goal
- Makes contingency plans

Supporting knowledge:
- Knows the vocabulary related to planning
- Is able to construct and implement a step-by-step plan for a given task
- Is able to predict possible problems
- Is able to identify ways to solve the problems through contingency plans
- Is able to complete a plan

What are the specific parts to this lesson? (In the order to be delivered.)

1. First, ask students if they have ever planned something only to have the plans not go well. Provide opportunities for students to talk about planning for a trip, to bake a cake, or to have a birthday party. Ask them what steps they took.

2. Read to the class *Mama Provi and the Pot of Rice,* by Sylvia Rosa-Casanova. In this book, Mama Provi lives in an apartment house on the first floor. Her granddaughter, Luci, lives on the eighth floor. When Luci gets the chicken pox, Mama Provi makes her famous *arroz con pollo* to take to her granddaughter. At each floor along the way, the wonderful aroma of her dish brings out the neighbors, who add to the meal. Ask the students if Mama Provi had a plan. Did her plan change as she went along? With your students plot Mama Provi's plan for her dinner with her granddaughter, floor by floor.

3. Tell the students that they will be starting a unit on planning and tell them the objectives in simple terms so that they know what they will be studying. Refer back to the

**Form 7.1**    Plan Books for Unit on Planning

My Plan Book

This unit is about planning. My personal goals for the learning are

1.

2.

3.

objectives throughout the lesson. Put the objectives somewhere in the room so that students can see them.

4. Pass out page one of a booklet on planning, which the students will complete throughout the unit. Ask students to put their names on their planning books and to draw on the front of their planning books to personalize the books (see Form 7.1).

5. Explain to students that their family members can help them with this unit. Write a letter to the parents telling them about the unit on planning, and give these letters to the students for their family members (see Form 7.2).

**Form 7.2**      Letter to Parents

---

Dear Families of Second-Graders

Our class is beginning a unit on how to make plans. Throughout the course of the unit, we will be addressing the following standards and benchmarks:

Standard 1: Sets and manages goals

Benchmark:

- Identifies resources necessary to complete a goal

- Displays a sense of personal direction and purpose

- Maintains an awareness of proximity to goal

- Makes contingency plans

Supporting knowledge:

- Knows the vocabulary related to planning

- Is able to construct and implement a step-by-step plan for a given task

- Is able to predict possible problems

- Is able to identify ways to solve the problems through contingency plans

We will be mastering these benchmarks over the course of a unit consisting of six lessons, which will last approximately two or three weeks.

- Lessons 1 and 2 teach students about what is meant by planning. Students will learn vocabulary related to planning. Students also will learn to create various types of plans and to think about how they used those plans to do their work.

- Lessons 3 and 4 teach students how to build thinking tools and when to use each one.

---

*(Continued)*

**Form 7.2** Continued

- Lesson 5 teaches students how planning is used in the real world.

- Lesson 6 provides students with an opportunity to use their planning books to plan for a project.

Throughout this unit, I encourage you to discuss the lessons and learning with your child. You may want to let your child help you with planning at home, such as grocery shopping and meal planning.

Sincerely,

6. Before introducing the vocabulary needed for this unit, pre-assess students' prior knowledge of planning, using the knowledge-rating scale entitled "What Do I Know?" (see Form 7.3). Tell students they may already know some information about the information they will learn in this unit. Model the process, using the first word or two, by thinking aloud (e.g., "Materials . . . hmmm, I think I know what this means, so I'll check 'Have Heard It/Seen It'"). For less proficient readers, pronounce the list of words so they do not have a problem decoding.

7. Tally how many students know (or think they know) each word and encourage discussion.

8. Using the introductory sheet from the students' planning books, guide students in setting personal goals for the lesson.

Carefully and consciously teaching vocabulary is critical to helping students' understanding of a subject. To teach vocabulary, use an instructional sequence that gives students multiple exposures to the words. Some ideas for teaching the vocabulary at this point include the following:

- Present students with a brief explanation or description of the new term or phrase. Use their planning books to point out where the word is used in planning.
- Present students with a nonlinguistic representation (e.g., a picture or drawing) of the new term or phrase. For example, for the term *gather*, you might show a picture of a student gathering materials to paint a watercolor. Or, you may decide to let students model the words by asking a student to go around the room and gather materials for a specific task.
- Ask students to generate their own explanations or descriptions of the term or phrase and write it in their planning book (see Form 7.4).

**Form 7.3**    What Do I Know?

| Word | Know It Well | Have Heard It/Seen It | Don't Know It |
|---|---|---|---|
| Planning | | | |
| Materials | | | |
| Gather | | | |
| Steps | | | |
| Problems | | | |
| Solve | | | |
| Evaluate | | | |

- Periodically and throughout the year, have students review their planning tools for accuracy.

How will I assess declarative knowledge for this lesson? I may:

**Form 7.4**    Teaching Vocabulary With Pictures

| Word | Definition | My Picture |
|------|------------|------------|
| Gather | | |
| Materials | | |
| Planning | | |
| Evaluation | | |

- Informally assess student's prior knowledge through the "What Do I Know?" activity.

How will I assess procedural knowledge for this lesson? I may:

- Assess student participation in the "What Do I Know?" activity as students share what they know.
- Observe students as they work in their planning books.
- Use the "How Am I Doing?" sheet in the planning book for students to informally reflect on their progress toward learning the standard and the benchmarks, as well as their progress toward their own goals (see Form 7.5).

**Form 7.5**    How Am I Doing?

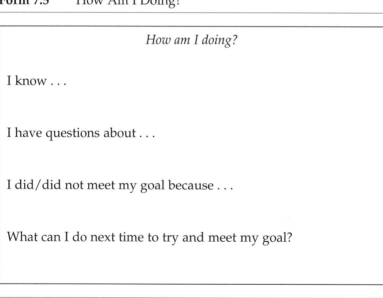

*How am I doing?*

I know . . .


I have questions about . . .


I did/did not meet my goal because . . .


What can I do next time to try and meet my goal?

- As an assessment guide, ask students to complete a planning worksheet for any tasks assigned (see Form 7.6).

As a final check, I will need to be sure that I have included all of the steps for learning declarative and procedural knowledge.

## DECLARATIVE KNOWLEDGE

What have I done to aid my students to construct meaning?

- We read a book in which the main character made a plan, and we discussed how she changed her plans as needed.
- My students set personal goals for the unit.
- My students completed a "What I Know" form prior to the learning using the given vocabulary words.
- My students were explicitly given the learning goals for the unit.
- My students were explicitly taught the vocabulary.

What have I done to aid my students to organize the information?

- My students were given the definitions and examples of the vocabulary words and then were asked to create their own definition and picture.
- Students completed a planning sheet that contained the words and the process.

What have I done to aid my students to put the information into long-term memory.

- The information was given a real-world context as we used the information to plan a task.
- Connections were made between what the students already know and the new knowledge through questions and drawings.

**Form 7.6**    Planning Worksheet

*Directions:* Draw what you are going to do.

Write or dictate the information:

| 1. Gather Materials | 2. | 3. |
|---|---|---|
| 4. | 5. | 6. |
| 7. | 8. | 9. Evaluate |

**Form 7.6** Continued

Sketch problems you could have.

Sketch how you could solve them.

- The students were exposed to auditory learning, visual learning (through seeing the vocabulary examples), and kinesthetic learning (by actually performing a task for which they planned).
- Students were given the opportunity to reflect on their learning and to draw conclusions about their own learning.

## Procedural Knowledge

What have I done to aid my students in constructing models?

- I provided definitions and examples of the vocabulary, and then my students wrote their own definitions and drew the process.

What have I done to aid my students in shaping the skills and processes?

- Through questioning techniques, I led my students through a process of finding examples of planning in the book that we read.
- I provided models for my students to see.
- I provided pictures for my students to view followed by their drawing their own models.

What have I done to aid my students in internalizing the process and skills?

- Students were given time to draw their own vocabulary symbols.
- Students were given the opportunity to use the planning process to complete a task.
- Students were given the opportunity to reflect on their learning and to measure where they are in terms of personal goals.

**Form 7.7**    Teacher Self-Assessment

As a teacher, reflect on your teaching and learning during this unit.

- What worked well in this unit? Why?

- What needs to be changed in this unit? Why?

- Suggestions for improving this unit.

  Was the amount of time I set aside for the unit adequate?

  Do I need more/less time for certain lessons?

  Which ones?

- I think my students really understand . . . because . . .

- I think my students do not understand . . . at all, because . . .

## REFLECTION

At the end of the unit, I will want students to have the opportunity to evaluate their learning in terms of the whole unit. I will also want to evaluate the unit in terms of the activities and processes. Form 7.7 is an example of what my self-assessment might look like.

# 8

# Building a Model for Planning

Using the flow chart in Figure 8.1 as a guide, let's review the steps involved in planning for the classroom and the guidelines that can help the classroom teacher evaluate his or her plans.

1. Use the state goals as a guide in deciding what to teach.

2. Write the state goal and any benchmarks that accompany that goal.

3. Decide what to teach from the goals provided.

4. Develop both declarative objectives (what will students know) and procedural objectives (what will students be able to do) for the learning.

5. Using the declarative and procedural objectives as a guide, decide how you will assess the learning. How will you know that students have learned the declarative information? How will you know that students can use

**Figure 8.1**   Planning Flow Chart

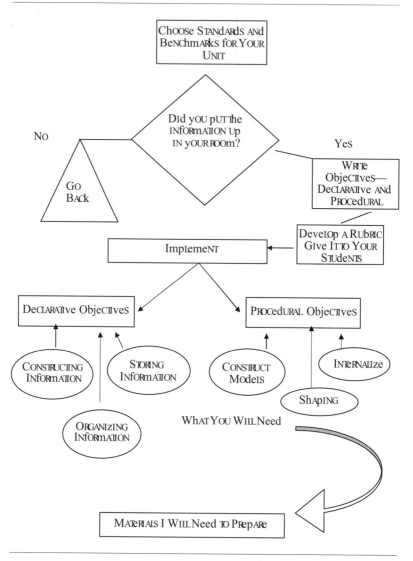

what they have learned or that they can perform the procedures taught?

6. Provide a matrix for your students showing the expectations for the learning. The matrix should directly reflect the objectives for the lesson.

7. At the elementary level, send home a letter telling parents the goals for the unit or lessons to be studied.

8. Place the objectives in the classroom so that they can be seen by the class. Refer to them often throughout the lesson or unit of study.

9. Ask students to write personal goals for the learning. Ask students to refer to their personal goals periodically and at the end of the lesson to determine if their goals were met.

10. Write lesson plans using the following questions as a guide:
   - How will students construct declarative information? How will you use prior knowledge and experiences of the students to help them interpret the new learning?
   - How will students organize declarative information? How will you help students to determine what is important and what is not? How will you help students to put the information into a linguistic or nonlinguistic model?
   - How will students store declarative information? How will the information be rehearsed so that it can easily be retrieved from storage?
   - How will students construct models for the procedural information? Will the initial model be constructed by the teacher or by the learner?
   - How will students use shaping for procedural information? Will adequate time and feedback be given so that students create ownership to their own model?
   - How will students internalize the procedural information? Will adequate time and feedback be given so that students use the model to the point that it is automatic?

11. What materials will you need to make this unit successful?

12. How will you evaluate your success in planning? Will you tie your evaluation to the results of your students' assessments?

# Vocabulary Summary

## Accountability

*Accountability* is the way in which an agency shows its clientele that it is accomplishing its mission and that it is fiscally responsible. In education, accountability is currently thought to require measurable proof, usually in the form of student success rates on various tests, that teachers, schools, districts, and states are teaching students efficiently and well.

Accountability in schools revolves around adopted state curriculum standards and assessments that measure those standards.

## Achievement Gap

An *achievement gap* occurs when there is a significant and persistent difference in the achievement among assorted groups or students as indicated on standardized tests, teacher grades, and other data identified by the state or governing entity. The gaps most frequently referred to are those between whites and minority groups, especially African Americans and Hispanics.

One way to find out if there is an achievement gap in your classroom is to disaggregate data on your students to see whether minority groups are making the same advances that you find with white students. In other words, if white students are making a 2% gain in reading, look to see that minority students are making at least the same gain. You can teach so that minorities make gains by using two tools: pluralizing and conceptualizing.

Another common achievement gap is the gap between students from poverty and middle-class students. The gap is not only in terms of standardized test scores, but also in terms of attendance, drop-out rates, and exposure to higher-level courses.

## Alignment

*Alignment* is the effort to ensure that what teachers teach is in accord with what the curriculum says will be taught and what is assessed on official tests. If students are not taught the intended content—because of inadequate learning materials, inadequate teacher preparation, or other reasons—or if official tests assess knowledge and skills different from those taught, test scores will obviously be lower than they otherwise would be. For this reason, schools and school districts often devote considerable attention to alignment.

## Assessment

*Assessment* is the act of measuring the learning and performance of students or teachers. Types of assessment instruments include achievement tests, minimum competency tests, developmental screening tests, aptitude tests, observation instruments, performance tasks, and authentic assessments.

The effectiveness of a particular approach to assessment depends on its suitability for the intended purpose. For instance, multiple-choice, true-or-false, and fill-in-the-blank tests can be used to assess basic skills or to find out what students remember. To assess other abilities, performance tasks may be more appropriate. According to Marzano (2001),

Performance assessments require students to perform a task, such as serving a volleyball, solving a particular type of mathematics problem, or writing a short business letter to inquire about a product. Sometimes the task may be designed to assess the student's ability to apply knowledge learned in school. For example, a student might be asked to determine what types of plants could be grown in various soil samples by measuring their pH levels.

## Benchmark

A *benchmark* is a standard for judging a performance. Some schools develop benchmarks to tell what students should know by a particular stage of their schooling: for example, "by the end of sixth grade, students should be able to locate major cities and other geographical features on each of the continents."
According to Marzano (2001),

Most state standards are written in broad terms such as, "K–2. Students will understand and apply basic and advanced properties of the concepts of geometry." The standard will then be broken down into benchmarks so that the teacher and students may know if they are teaching and learning that standard.

As an example, Marzano offers possible benchmarks for a standard on geometry:

Benchmark: Understands basic properties (e.g., number of sides, corners, square corners) of and similarities and differences between simple geometric shapes.

Benchmark: Understands the common language of spatial sense (e.g., inside, between, above, below, behind).

## Cognitive Development

*Cognitive development* refers to the process, which begins at birth, of learning through sensory perception, memory, and observation. Children are born into cultures and backgrounds that affect both what they learn and how they learn. Children from enriched environments (in which parents and caregivers read to and with them, teach them letters and numbers, and take them to plays and museums) come to school prepared to learn; children from impoverished or abusive backgrounds often lack most of all of these preschool advantages. To stimulate the cognitive development of such children, teachers use such strategies as placing learning into a meaningful context, providing situations in which students can be active participants, and combining general information with specific learning situations.

## Contextualizing

*Contextualizing* information is the process of putting it into a framework, such as a story format. For many of our learners, this is the way they learn best, because it is the way that the culture from which they come learns new information. If you teach students from poverty or Hispanic or African American students, it is important that you put information into context for them. Teaching them declarative information in a traditional format, such as discussion or lecture, will make it more difficult for them to give meaning to the learning than if the information is taught in a context, such as a story or situation.

## Cooperative Learning

*Cooperative learning* is a teaching strategy combining teamwork with individual and group accountability. Working in small groups composed of individuals of varying talents, abilities, and backgrounds, students are given one or more tasks. The teacher or the group often assigns each team member a personal responsibility that is essential to the successful completion of the task.

Used well, cooperative learning allows students to acquire both knowledge and social skills. The students learn from one another and get to know and respect group members that they may not have made an effort to meet in other circumstances. Studies show that, when used properly, cooperative learning boosts student achievement. Schools using this strategy report that attendance improves, because the students feel valuable and necessary to their group.

## Curriculum

Although the term *curriculum* has many possible meanings, it usually refers to a written plan outlining what students will be taught (i.e., a course of study). Curriculum documents often also include detailed directions or suggestions for teaching the content. *Curriculum* may refer to all the courses offered at a given school or all the courses offered at a school in a particular area of study. For example, the English curriculum might include English literature, literature, world literature, essay styles, creative writing, business writing, Shakespeare, modern poetry, and the novel. The curriculum of an elementary school usually includes language arts, mathematics, science, social studies, and other subjects.

## Data-Based Decision Making

*Data-based decision making* involves analyzing existing sources of information, such as class and school attendance rates, drop-out rates, grades, test scores, portfolios, surveys, and interviews, to make decisions about the school or classroom. The process involves organizing and interpreting the data and creating action plans.

## Declarative Information Related to Storage

Declarative information is the most difficult learning for the brain to store. The three necessary processes students use to process declarative information and send it to long-term memory are (1) constructing meaning, (2) organizing information, and (3) storing declarative information.

*Constructing Meaning.* If the learning does not make sense or does not have meaning to the learner, there is a high probability the learner will tune out the information. Each of us constructs meaning for ourselves; no one can do it for us.

There are, however, some things that a teacher can do to help students construct meaning. Teachers can begin lessons by hooking old learning to new learning. The brain likes patterns and always looks for information that it already has stored to hook onto new information. If you are teaching a unit in which students do not have prior learning, try to build empathy or a personal attachment to the new learning by asking questions or providing simulations to help students connect to the characters or information. For example, in introducing a unit on estimation, you might bring in a jar of marbles and have a contest to see who can guess how many marbles are in the jar. Let students work in small groups and compete for the correct answer. Then ask them to talk about the mental processes that they used to come up with their answer.

*Organizing Information.* As mentioned, the brain likes patterns. Anything that the teacher can do to help students see patterns to organize their information will help them to remember it. The outline is the most common way of doing this, but it is not a brain-compatible strategy for many students. Nonlinguistic organizers have a superior effect on helping students to organize and remember information. Such organizers can simply show the attributes of a given subject or they can use much more sophisticated thinking. For example, at a beginning level, a teacher might directly teach and demonstrate to the students how to make a simple circle graph that shows a chain of events leading to a conclusion (see Figure V.1 for a simple circle graph of the events that led to the Boston Tea Party). As a teacher, if I want my students to begin to see the interconnectedness of events, I might expand on this basic model to show students how side events affect the major events. Figure V.2 is an example of how that model might look. This model shows not only the sequence of events, but side issues that affected the main sequence. The point is that we can lead students into pretty sophisticated thinking through models. For more information on how to use higher-level models in the classroom, go to www.pegasuscom.com.

**Figure V.1**    Simple Circle Graph Showing Events in Order

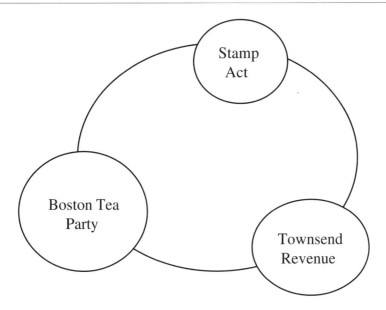

*Storing Declarative Information.* The storage pathway for factual information is the semantic memory system, which is the least reliable of all the memory pathways. If you have had the experience of trying to recall something that you are sure you know but can't seem to remember, the chances are that it is factual information you are seeking. Storing this information does not mean that you will be able to recall it easily. Semantic memory needs a connector or hook to help embed the information and to help you to remember. We give students hooks by utilizing other memory systems. For example, by adding movement to the learning, we use the procedural memory system, which is very good at remembering. By color-coding to vocabulary sheets or using graphic models, we add context to the learning and use the episodic memory system. By adding emotion in the form of music, discussions, or debates, we use the emotional memory system of the brain. Putting interest, excitement, and challenge into the learning all help embed and strengthen the learning and recall.

**Figure V.2**    Complex Circle Graph Showing How Events Are
Interrelated

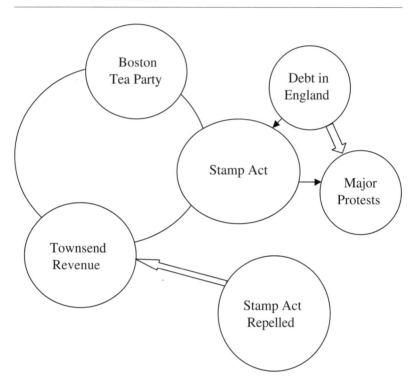

## Declarative Objectives

*Declarative objectives* are developed around what teachers want
students to know as a result of the instructional process: These
are the facts and information in the learning. For example, two
declarative objectives might be as follows:

- Students will know the steps necessary for problem
  solving.
- Students will know the vocabulary for the unit of study.

## Enrichment

*Enrichment* refers to topics and activities that are valuable and
interesting to learn, but are not basic education—knowledge

that is "nice to know," but not necessarily what people need to know. Although people will not necessarily agree on what is basic and what is enrichment, examples might include a study of Wordsworth's poetry or a biography of Alexander Hamilton.

The term *enrichment* is also applied to efforts that parents make to supplement their children's learning outside of school, such as trips to science and art museums, educational vacations, visits to local libraries, and attendance at local theaters, orchestras, or ballets.

## Essential Questions

*Essential questions* are basic questions—such as "What is distinctive about the American experience?"—used to provide focus for a course or a unit of study. Such questions need to be derived from vitally important themes and topics, and their answers cannot be summarized neatly and concisely.

## Explicit Instruction

*Explicit instruction* is a teacher-directed strategy that includes such methods as lecture, didactic questioning, drill and practice exercises, and demonstrations to learn specific skill information or the steps involved with a process.

The steps involved in explicit instruction include, first, the offering by the teacher of controlled examples and practice activities guided by the teacher and including examples and nonexamples (examples of what something is not).

Next, students are involved in guided practice activities, in which students practice the learning with the teacher present to give immediate feedback. Third, students are moved to independent practice, where they practice the learning without the teacher present as they work (e.g., homework).

In explicit instruction, the teacher makes the thought processes used for successful reading and writing as transparent as possible through explanation, demonstration, guided practice, and feedback. First, the teacher names and explains *what* the strategy is, tells students *why* the strategy is helpful, and shows the learners *when* and *how* to apply the strategy for the tasks. Second, the teacher provides scaffolding opportunities for the learners to practice applying the strategy and encourages the learners to self-assess the effectiveness of their strategy use.

## Indirect Experience

Students experience declarative information (e.g., concepts, generalizations, principles, facts, and vocabulary) either directly or indirectly in the classroom. A *direct experience* is one in which students are involved in physical activity. The physical involvement can be real or simulated. For example, a real experience of an airplane ride would involve going up in an airplane, whereas a simulated experience might involve riding in a flight simulator or setting up a mock airplane in the classroom.

An *indirect experience* is one in which students are not involved in physical activity. Common indirect experiences include observation, demonstrations, watching films, reading, and listening to presentations or lectures. Because they require relatively little time and energy to set up, indirect experiences are most commonly used in the classroom, but a teacher should try to use a mix of direct and indirect experiences whenever possible.

## Interdisciplinary Curriculum

An *interdisciplinary curriculum* draws its content from two or more subject areas to focus on a particular topic or theme. Rather than studying literature and social studies separately, for example, a class might study a unit called "The Sea," in which students read poems and stories about people who spend their lives on or near the ocean, learn about the geography of coastal area, and investigate why coastal and inland populations have different livelihoods. Effective interdisciplinary studies have the following elements:

- A topic that lends itself to study from several points of view
- One or more themes (or essential questions) the teacher wants the students to explore
- Activities intended to further students' understanding by establishing relationships among knowledge from more than one discipline or school subject

Interdisciplinary curriculum, which draws content from particular disciplines that are ordinarily taught separately, is different from *integrated curriculum*, which involves investigation of topics without regard to where, or even to whether, they appear in the typical school curriculum at all.

## Mixed-Ability Grouping

Intentionally mixing students of varying talents and needs in the same classroom is called *mixed-ability grouping*. The success of this method, also called *heterogeneous grouping*, depends on the teacher's skill in differentiating instruction so that all students feel challenged and successful. Advocates say mixed-ability grouping prevents lower-track classes from becoming dumping grounds and ensures that all students have access to high-status content. Opponents say it is difficult for teachers to manage, hampers the brightest students from moving at an accelerated pace, and contributes to a watered-down curriculum.

## Multi-Age Grouping

*Multi-age grouping* is the practice of having children of different ages in the same classroom, rather than assigning them to age-graded classrooms (e.g., assigning six-year-old children to the first grade and seven-year-old children to the second grade). Multi-age grouping is practiced more often in elementary schools than in secondary schools. Typical multi-age groupings are children ages 5 to 7 as primary students and children ages 8 to 10 as intermediate students. The reason for combining two or more grade levels is to group students with others who are at the same developmental level, regardless of age. In other words, students can learn at a faster or slower pace without being made to feel abnormal.

## Performance Tasks

*Performance tasks* are activities, exercises, or problems that require students to show what they can do. Some performance tasks are intended to assess a skill, such as solving a particular type of mathematical problem. Others are designed to have students demonstrate their understanding by applying knowledge. For example, students might be given a current political map of Africa showing the names and locations of countries and a similar map from 1945 and be asked to explain the differences and similarities. To be more authentic (more like the real world), the task might be to prepare a newspaper article explaining the changes.

Performance tasks often have more than one acceptable solution. They may call on a student to create a response to a problem and then explain or defend it. Performance tasks are considered a type of assessment (used instead of, or in addition to, conventional tests), but they may also be used as learning activities.

## Pluralizing

*Pluralizing* is the act of providing at least three strategies for teaching information to students. For example, a teacher might directly teach a vocabulary word by providing its definition and examples. He might also provide context to the vocabulary word by telling a story or having students provide stories that illustrate the meaning of the word. Third, he might have students use a chart, such as the one in Table V.1, to have students draw a symbol to help them remember the word.

The first strategy for teaching the vocabulary is a traditional method used in most middle-class classrooms, where the students speak English as their primary language. The second

**Table V.1**     Model for Teaching Vocabulary to Students

| Vocabulary Word | Definition | Sketch |
|---|---|---|
| | A figure having four equal sides | Square <br> □ |

example is one that might be used for students from urban areas who have grown up in poverty. Giving the word a context is important to them because that is how they learn in their environment; since they do not use the formal language of the middle class, giving a context to the word will help to give it meaning. The last example might be used to help English language learners (ELLs), who do not have the vocabulary to give context to the learning. By providing visual models for them, the teacher helps them to store the information in the contextual pathway (i.e., episodic memory) rather than struggling to store it in the semantic pathway, which is word- and fact-dominant.

## Procedural Objectives

*Procedural objectives* are those things we want students to be able to do as a result of the learning. Procedural objectives deal with skills and processes. There are four questions that the teacher needs to ask as she prepares procedural objectives for a unit or lesson:

*Which skills and processes do students really need to master?* Marzano (1992) says, "Direct attention to model building, shaping, and internalizing should be reserved for those skills and processes that are very important to the content, highly complex, or unfamiliar to students." For example, for a unit on weather, a teacher might determine that it is important for students to know how to read a barometer. This is a skill that they will use throughout life and that is important in determining temperature as they study about weather changes. It is important to note that not all of the skills used in a lesson may be worthy of mastery at this point and thus would not be a part of the procedural objectives for the lesson. They may be nice to know, but are not essential.

The next three questions relate to the processes that students use to put procedural information into long-term memory.

*How will students be aided in constructing models?* Some ways that the teacher can help students construct models is by thinking aloud so that students see the process the teacher goes through in making decisions about the process, by providing a written set of steps for students, and by using flow charts. Creating mental pictures of the learning is also an effective method of using models. For example, an elementary teacher may ask students to mentally go through the steps of creating a collage. Or a literature teacher may provide students with the steps to create a limerick; as she reads through each step, she gives the students an example. A math teacher may demonstrate the process of long division, allow time for the students to practice, and then ask students to create a flow chart of the steps involved.

*How will students be aided in shaping the skill or process?* (See *Shaping.*) Shaping is the most overlooked part of learning procedural knowledge, thus overt planning for it is critical.

*How will students be aided in internalizing the skill or process?* Practice is the key to internalizing procedural knowledge. How much time will be spent in practice (including massed and distributed practice)? In general, practice periods should initially be spaced close together and then gradually spaced further and further apart. For example, a reading teacher may provide daily activities for students to locate reference materials. After developing some ability at locating reference materials, students practice for 30 minutes a day on both Monday and Tuesday, and then again for 30 minutes on Friday. During the next week, they have two 30-minute periods of practice. In the three following weeks, they have one 30-minute period of practice each week.

## Reflection Activities

*Reflection activities* are those activities that lead students to think about the learning and to identify what they have learned as well as what they still do not understand. Using reflection exercises after the learning helps students to put the information into long-term memory. Reflection gives owner-ship to the learning and assures that students will do mental processing.

Some tools that are used in reflection include the KWLH (Know, Want to know, Learned, How I learned) exercise. Some other tools include the PMI (Positive-Minus-Interesting); What, So What, and Now What; and Ticket Out the Door.

## Scaffolding

*Scaffolding* is the way a teacher provides support to make sure students succeed at complex tasks they couldn't do otherwise. Most teaching is done as the students go about a task, rather than before they start. For example, as a group of elementary students proceed to publish a student newspaper, the teacher shows them how to conduct interviews, write news stories, and prepare captions for photographs. Because the teacher *supports* the students to make sure they don't fail in their effort, researchers use the image of the scaffolding that workers sometimes place around buildings. As the students become more skillful, the teacher gives them more responsibility, taking way the scaffolding when it is no longer needed. This gradual withdrawal has been called *fading*.

## Shaping

Shaping is one of the three processes necessary for procedural information to be placed into long-term memory. *Shaping* refers to the involvement of the learner in the process, which makes the process the learner's own. When students construct an initial model for a new skill or process, they usually start with one model but shape it and change it until it becomes workable for them. For example, a student may construct an initial model for performing long division, but will later discover some shortcuts and tricks that make the process work better for him. These changes are called *shaping*. Marzano (1992) says,

> The importance of shaping a new skill or process cannot be exaggerated. Teachers' inattention to this aspect of learning procedural knowledge is a primary reason for students' failure to effectively use basic skills and processes. Classroom activities for shaping must be planned.

Some ways that the teacher can plan for shaping include

- Providing opportunities for students to practice the learning. As they practice, help them to see the variations in the process. For example, a writing teacher talks through the process that he uses as he writes to help students shape the process. He works on an essay shown on an overhead projector: "Let's see, should I use the pronoun 'you' or 'one' here? If I use 'one', then I pretty much have to stay with it throughout the essay. . . ."
- Pointing out common errors and pitfalls. It is easy for errors to creep into a skill or process when students are first learning it. Consequently, one aspect of shaping procedural knowledge is to point out errors and pitfalls to students. The teacher can demonstrate these common errors and pitfalls, or she can point out errors as students make them.
- Providing a variety of situations in which students use a specific skill or process. Most skills or processes important to a given content area can be used in a variety of settings. For example, the process of long division is used

in many different ways in many types of problems. An important part of shaping is allowing students to experience a variety of situations in which the skill or process being learned might be used.

## Spiral Curriculum

*Spiral curriculum* is a curriculum design that provides for periodic revisiting of key topics over a period of years, presenting them in greater depth each time. Thus the objectives change each time the material is reintroduced so that they are developmentally appropriate and so that the learning becomes more in-depth with each spiral. Spiral curriculum contrasts with *mastery learning,* which assumes that a topic should be taught thoroughly and mastered before students move on to something else.

## Standards

In current usage, *standards* usually refers to specific criteria for what students are expected to learn and be able to do. These standards usually take two forms in the curriculum:

- *Content standards* that tell what students are expected to know and be able to do in various subject areas, such as mathematics and science.
- *Performance standards* that specify what levels of learning are expected. Performance standards assess the degree to which content standards have been met.

We currently have national and state standards. Many areas have local standards as well. All of these should be aligned with each other.

## Teaching for Understanding

Engaging students in learning activities intended to help them understand the complexities of a topic is referred to as *teaching for understanding.* Teaching for understanding is different from teaching simply for recall, which results in students being able to answer questions without knowing what their answers really mean. Specialists advise that a good way to know whether students understand is to ask them to perform a task that shows they can apply and make use in a realistic setting of what they have learned. For example, students might participate in a mock trial to demonstrate that they have developed their understanding of the rights of the accused. When students perform a task to show application and understanding, we call it a *performance task.*

## Teaching to the Test

*Teaching to the test* occurs when teachers prepare students for a test by concentrating on the particular things the test contains rather than on the broader body of knowledge the test is intended to measure. An extreme example would be drilling students on the 20 words the teacher knows will appear on a spelling test rather than teaching the whole set of words students are supposed to have learned to spell.

# Vocabulary
# Post-Test

At the beginning of this book, you were given a vocabulary list and a pre-test on that vocabulary. Below are the post-test and the answer key for the vocabulary assessment.

## VOCABULARY POST-TEST

**Instructions:** For each question, choose the one best answer.

1. Teaching the 20 words that will be on the spelling test to the exclusion of other spelling words is called . . .
   A. Teaching to the test
   B. Teaching for understanding
   C. Shaping
   D. Explicit teaching

2. A lesson is aligned when . . .
   A. We teach for understanding
   B. We teach to the objectives
   C. We teach and assess to the written curriculum or standards
   D. We use state and local standards as a base for learning

3. What is the term for teaching the same concepts over time with each introduction adding depth to the learning?
   A. Scaffolding
   B. Spiral curriculum

    C. Performance tasks

    D. Teaching for understanding

4. When we look at data to determine if all groups of students are making gains in learning, we have . . .
   A. Differentiated the data
   B. Benchmarked the data
   C. Disaggregated the data
   D. Manipulated the data

5. Essential questions relate to . . .
   A. Dividing units into lessons
   B. Good questioning techniques
   C. Declarative objectives
   D. Procedural objectives

6. Providing opportunities for bright students to work on more complex tasks is called what?
   A. Scaffolding
   B. Performance tasks
   C. Enrichment
   D. Pluralizing

7. Choose the answer that is *not* an example of a phase of procedural knowledge.
   A. Constructing models
   B. Meaning making
   C. Shaping
   D. Internalizing

8. What is the most overlooked phase of procedural knowledge?
   A. Constructing models
   B. Meaning making
   C. Shaping
   D. Internalizing

9. What is the key to internalizing?
   A. Practice
   B. Modeling

C. Extending

D. Questioning

10. When we point out to students possible problems they may encounter in the learning, we are using . . .
    A. Extending
    B. Modeling
    C. Shaping
    D. Organizing

11. Nonlinguistic or graphic models are an example of what?
    A. Shaping
    B. Organizing
    C. Extending
    D. Internalizing

12. Giving students many examples and ideas and then gradually giving less directions as students have more opportunities to use the information is an example of . . .
    A. Organizing
    B. Internalizing
    C. Shaping
    D. Scaffolding

13. *Resources, group goals, environment,* and *tasks* are terms used in . . .
    A. Enrichment
    B. Cooperative learning
    C. Differentiated instruction
    D. Interdisciplinary curriculum

14. Which of the pathways is most often used in providing context to the learning?
    A. Procedural
    B. Semantic
    C. Episodic
    D. Automatic

15. Teaching by using a story format is an example of what?
    A. Pluralizing
    B. Contextualizing
    C. Scaffolding
    D. Enrichment

16. When we add movement to learning math facts, we are adding which of the pathways to the learning?
    A. Semantic
    B. Episodic
    C. Enriching
    D. Procedural

17. An example of a procedural objective is . . .
    A. "Students will know the meaning of the vocabulary."
    B. "Students will develop a plan for problem solving."
    C. "Students will know the names of the main characters in the story."
    D. "Students will know the parts to a story."

18. An example of a declarative objective is . . .
    A. "Students will know the parts to a story."
    B. "Students will answer the questions asked by their peers."
    C. "Students will develop a mind map on the parts of a bicycle."
    D. "Students will demonstrate variations and errors."

19. Teachers who provide more than one context when teaching are . . .
    A. Scaffolding
    B. Pluralizing
    C. Using spiral curriculum
    D. Using direct experience

20. Which of the following is *not* true of performance tasks?
    A. They are written for a given audience.
    B. They are real world.
    C. They are procedural.
    D. They are usually teacher driven.

## VOCABULARY POST-TEST ANSWER KEY

| | | | |
|---|---|---|---|
| 1. | A | 11. | B |
| 2. | C | 12. | D |
| 3. | B | 13. | B |
| 4. | C | 14. | C |
| 5. | A | 15. | B |
| 6. | C | 16. | A |
| 7. | B | 17. | B |
| 8. | C | 18. | A |
| 9. | A | 19. | B |
| 10. | C | 20. | D |

# References

Anderson, J. (1990). *Cognitive psychology and its implications.* New York: W. H. Freeman.

Bandler, R. (1988). *Learning strategies: Acquisition and conviction* [Videotape]. Boulder, CO: NLP Comprehensive.

Jensen, E. (1997). *Completing the puzzle: The brain-compatible approach to learning* (2nd ed.). Del Mar, California: Turning Point.

Marzano, R. J. (1992). *A different kind of classroom: Teaching with dimensions of learning.* Alexandria, VA: Association for Supervision and Curriculum Development.

Marzano, R .J. (1998). *A theory-based meta-analysis of research on instruction.* Aurora, CO: Mid-Continent Regional Educational Laboratory.

Marzano, R. J. (2001). *Designing a new taxonomy of educational objectives.* Thousand Oaks, CA: Corwin.

Parks, S., & Black, H. (1992). *Organizing thinking* (Vol. 1). Pacific Grove, CA: Critical Thinking Press.

Snowman, J., & McCown, R. (1984, April). *Cognitive processes in learning: A model of investigating strategies and tactics.* Paper presented at the annual meeting of the American Educational Research Association, New Orleans, LA.

Sprenger, M. (2002). *Becoming a wiz at brain-based teaching: How to make every year your best year.* Thousand Oaks, CA: Corwin.

Tileston, D. W. (2004a). *What every teacher should know about diverse learners.* Thousand Oaks, CA: Corwin.

Tileston, D. W. (2004b). *What every teacher should know about student assessment.* Thousand Oaks, CA: Corwin.

Tileston, D. W. (2004c). *What every teacher should know about student motivation.* Thousand Oaks, CA: Corwin.

Wiggins, G., & McTighe, J. (1998). *Understanding by design.* Alexandria, VA: Association for Supervision and Curriculum Development.

# Index

**CORWIN
PRESS**

The Corwin Press logo—a raven striding across an open book—represents the happy union of courage and learning. We are a professional-level publisher of books and journals for K-12 educators, and we are committed to creating and providing resources that embody these qualities. Corwin's motto is "Success for All Learners."